What Is It About

Reflections and Explorations in Wonder and Bemusement

Arthur B. Weissman

"What Is It About: Reflections and Explorations in Wonder and Bemusement," by Arthur B. Weissman. ISBN 978-1-949756-47-0 (softcover); 978-1-949756-48-7 (eBook).

To Rebecca, Joseph, and Lowell

Contents

Author's Note (especially to grammarians): In many cases in these writings the plural version of the third-person possessive pronoun (i.e., "their") is used even for a singular subject instead of the multi-gender expression, "his/her." This follows colloquial usage and avoids constant repetition of an awkward (if politically correct) phrase.

A Path in the Woods

WHAT IS IT ABOUT a path in the woods that focuses my gaze to the near exclusion of more natural objects around it?

It doesn't have to be the old King's Highway in a New England forest, or the Appalachian Trail in the Shenandoahs. In fact, the latest object of my fixation is a sewer right-of-way through woodland in suburban Virginia, with incongruous manholes and pipes bumping up several times down the sight line. Yet, I eagerly anticipate looking down this "path" as I walk along the main trail.

Is it – despite my professed preference for nature – an instinctive attraction to a human-made form, one that facilitates passage through nature's thickets? Is it an interest in the history of land use, the more interesting the more faded and grown-up (though still identifiable) the path is? Or is it, as I suppose half in jest to myself, a metaphor for life – the path taken or not taken?

Certainly, woodlands and their trails and paths abound in our literature and mythology to represent life's journeys, hardships, and challenges. They are a favorite of allegories, and often the most fearsome things happen in the woods, usually along a path. One might think it safer, in fact, to digress from the path, but that introduces new dangers of being lost, falling into a bog, or confronting Sasquatch far from any help.

A clear path brings comfort to the hiker, much more than bivouacking through difficult terrain. But if the path is too much cleared, too wide or graded, much less paved, the joy is diminished or lost. A clear path, used but not worn, ensures that one is not likely to get lost. It is a helpful guide, impersonal though decidedly human. (In contrast, a deer path piques some interest but not the desire to follow it very far, if that is even possible.)

So, at the very least, the path in the woods is our security, the string leading to or from civilization we depend on and need to get away from at times. But is it ever more?

To answer this question it is useful to compare the allure of a road, which is the equivalent path for a vehicle through the countryside. The twentieth century, the car century, created a number of myths and romances around both the car and the road which it takes. Entire television shows (e.g., "Route 66") were centered on the road and the picaresque that it generated. An appealing road and a car to take on it promised adventure, calculated danger, and perhaps love fulfilled. Every American teen yearned to earn their license to partake of these treats that a road might offer.

In different geographies this allure of a road plays out in various ways, but always positively. A straight road in open country out West entrains the mind to think beyond the farthest distance, raising infinite possibilities, as the West has always done. A winding road in the Eastern woodlands bathes the mind in more soothing pastoral notions, wherein good things could lie ahead. And a narrow country road, such as an English country lane barely wide enough for a vehicle, evokes pleasant domestic feelings, with a tinge of the unknown.

A path in the woods is none of these, but it partakes of all. Our limited sight ahead provides unlimited possibilities to come, even when we know a trail fairly well. Each turn in the path opens up a new vista, a new biotic community, and the chance to see some kind of wildlife. That a path opens before us gives comfort we are going where others have and we will not be lost. As with a road, however, there is no guarantee we won't be led astray, out of our way, or into a dangerous place where we are not wanted or want to be. We may, indeed, want to get off the path – something we cannot do easily with a vehicle – or return the way we came.

A path in the woods gives recurrent pleasure of the unknown that a road experienced in a vehicle cannot do. It is virtually impossible to completely know a woodland, no matter the size or how many times we traverse it. (Ecologists studying the woods often restrict their purview to small plots of less than an acre.) That's why we can enjoy the same trail countless times, and see new things all the time, even apart from wildlife sightings, which are always spontaneous. A vehicle on a road allows limited immersion in the contemporaneous landscape, even for the passenger, and then it is on to the next limited view, so that one quickly tires of seeing "the same thing" over and over.

Yet, I said at the beginning that the path steals my attention from the woods around it. And so it does, but not completely. I have, after all, to make sure I don't stumble over rock or root, or miss a snake in the path ahead. I also gravitate to the human place in the woods, my security, from which I may more comfortably look out at the woods around me. Indeed, I must consciously look around and sometimes force myself to stop, to look to the sides and not just ahead up the trail.

I have not looked around enough over the years. Yes, I have stopped to "smell the roses," and much else likewise, as I always admire nature around me (and good cityscapes) in most any undegraded form. But taking a whiff, even a long look, over several hours, days, or even weeks (on vacation), does not free us enough from the conveyor belt of employment and family life. The mind loosens up somewhat and enlarges its otherwise narrow and overly focused attention. It cannot, however, ruminate sufficiently to discover new sources of fragrance, the rhythm of an entirely different natural system, or even the answer to a long-held puzzle that was staring one right in the face.

I experienced this change in perception during a break from decades-long employment in mostly office-based work. I saw animal action in the backyard I rarely observed before. I took care of a long-term medical problem that, in actuality, helped bring back the roses and more. And I noticed features and phenomena around the home, incontestably mundane but relevant to daily life, that had escaped my notice and understanding.

A close friend and fine naturalist in rural Connecticut does his "birding" by staying in one place and watching what comes through, rather than walking through the woods or fields hoping to see wildlife in those discrete moments in each place. I would like to set up along a trail, just off it perhaps, and watch everything around me for a long time. That would keep me from feeling as though I'm on a road, passing through rich terrain I hardly perceive much less understand. I would let the "through-hikers" practically running along the trail pass, let them achieve their records going up the mountain, while I indulge in the riches they leave behind.

On the trail, then, I am both driven and resisting, conforming to my civilized self and trying desperately to break away from it. I must look ahead down the trail, and also slow up to look around. I may digress from the trail a portion of the time, but readily return as it grows dark.

Yet still, overall, I will tend to look forward, up the path in the woods, anticipating always something new and interesting ahead that I cannot now see. This frame of mind is fundamentally different from looking around; it is a driver for much of our life, which we live in a time-driven forward, linear path mostly of hope. It motivates us to do things we might otherwise neglect, while also causing us to neglect things we might otherwise appreciate. This is what focuses my gaze on the path in the woods ahead, and I am loath to give it up.

Life's Mysteries

WHAT IS IT ABOUT life that it is so full of mysteries and unanswered questions?

When I was an inquisitive and naïve adolescent, I wondered aloud (in the school newspaper) how there could be so much news, which confronted me every morning on the kitchen table. I reasoned that the complexity of society and life produced this endless stream of happenings. In posing the current question, I wonder whether it is also truly naïve. Why wouldn't there be myriad mysteries in a universe that developed from mysterious beginnings almost fourteen billion years ago and evolved in complex ways astronomically, geologically, and biologically since? Why, indeed, would I presume that humans would necessarily understand all of this?

The issue becomes one of equilibration, balancing the complexity of the universe against the evolved intelligence of humans. So far, the balance has tipped heavily in the direction of the universe. We have certainly made inroads, particularly in the past several centuries with the scientific revolution. But each discovery seems to lead to more mysteries, and the larger ones about existence remain so. Every time science (primarily physics) claims to have solved the riddles of the universe, a new line of inquiry soon opens up. Can we conjecture that we will ever solve all of life's mysteries, physical or otherwise?

Of course, another view is that humans have a unique capacity to understand life's mysteries. That we have evolved to the point of doing so in many complex fields speaks to the miracle that is us. This attitude crops up curiously among some highly intelligent people, including ones who have unlocked some of nature's secrets. If I had their credits, I would probably crow as well. But, as wondrous as it is that the human brain has evolved to this level, it smacks a bit of arrogance to celebrate quite yet.

An alternative way to frame the question, then, is to ask why the world is so complex and secretive that humans, even with considerable cognitive development, cannot understand so much of it. Most of the answers to mysteries we have solved are hidden and not transparent. What is it about life's phenomena that makes their workings not apparent to the human eye or just plain difficult for us to understand?

Putting aside the origin of the universe, it may not always have been so complex. After the reputed Big Bang, scientists believe that the universe consisted only of simpler physical components such as subatomic particles and then, within the first million years as atoms formed, primarily hydrogen and helium. As stars began to form (believed to be after a half-billion more years!), heavier elements come into creation with the potential for new materials and, ultimately, life itself (through carbon, water, and other essential elements). But this picture is also riddled with mysteries, such as possibly different physical laws in force, superheated plasma states affecting behavior, and the existence of "antimatter" and "dark matter" that may have shaped the subsequent universe. And this does not even account for the very beginning, the Big Bang and so-called inflationary period right after when the universe emerged out of a point and expanded hugely within an infinitesimal part of a second.

As puzzling as contemporary cosmology may be, past discoveries must have caused astonishment as well. As the atomic theory emerged in the nineteenth and early twentieth centuries, people learned that so-called solid matter is not so – it is actually a conglomeration of tiny particles that are mostly empty space (core nuclei with tiny electrons spinning around them). As a young student learning about atoms, one goes through a similar stage of awe. Quantum theory clouded the picture even more, giving only probabilities for the location of electrons and postulating them as both particles and waves. More recent discoveries in particle physics have given us a menu of strange-named particles and forces, and now we confront the possibility that matter is just a bunch of strings in numerous dimensions. Then there is relativity, which warped our sense of space by showing that it can be bent by gravity, yet another mysterious force.

Our discoveries in biology and biochemistry have been equally striking. The evolution of living organisms seems so miraculous that some still cling to the idea that it has been divinely guided and could not have happened by chance and natural selection. At the individual level, each organism is a complex entity comprised of cells undergoing myriad physical and chemical functions within and among themselves. The more we learn about these processes, the more involved they seem. The mechanisms for cell reproduction and for transmission of genetic information through DNA represent both a triumph in human understanding and cause for human awe at how intricately but efficiently nature works. At the macro level, we are just beginning to understand the social communities of other animal species, how they communicate and how they interact. Nor do we have a complete understanding of the behaviors of most other species. In regard to one of the most basic behaviors, reproduction, do we know what (besides hormones) motivates and guides almost all animal species to *care for* their young so deliberately and competently?

Putting all the organisms together with their environment, we have the field of ecology, which has a long way to go to achieve similar understanding of its subject but has illuminated many fascinating interactions to date. We have come to appreciate the critical role of "lowly" bacteria and organisms in the soil, the complex flows of energy and matter in ecosystems, the role of predators in maintaining populations, and the web of interacting species and matter that is so resilient but also vulnerable to disruption and destruction. We have learned just how big an impact humans have had on ecosystems, and how much bigger that impact can now be with advanced industrialization and overpopulation. Climate change is just the latest of the large-scale impacts humans have caused, but unfortunately, it is potentially the largest and most devastating for the planet and its ecosystems.

I suspect my younger brethren would feel this list of accomplishments and wonders misses the greatest – "information technology," or all the information, communications, and control systems brought to us by computers and their assorted platforms. Indeed, this is a revolution in human culture, brought about by an understanding of physical technologies that are cleverly harnessed to process and transmit numerical, verbal, and visual data streams. The application of IT to many fields has already transformed our ability to understand and function in them. One of the more exciting developments on the horizon will be the conversion to self-driving vehicles, with the chance to save millions of human lives (and at some point, hopefully, wild animals' lives). All this surely warrants bragging about, as long as the result is beneficial for society and individual humans. Whether the development of artificial intelligence through computers follows in this direction remains unclear.

At this point we should consider the contribution of the humanities both to understanding some of life's mysteries and to uncovering more of them. If the sciences described above deal mostly with physical phenomena, the humanities – literature, philosophy, the arts – focus more on the human mind and spirit and their relationship to the world around them. As such, a central question in the humanities has always been the nature of existence and the place of humans in it. In this exploratory mode, the arts also delve into the wonders and mysteries of life, sometimes celebrating them, sometimes anguishing over the perplexity they cause. While no humanistic approach can ever be proved as a scientific theorem can, many perspectives provided by the humanities have given us invaluable insight into ourselves and our world and enriched the meaning of our lives. As with science, these perspectives often lead to further questions and mysteries. That has certainly been the result of many of the inquiries in this book.

Another key question in the humanities has been the nature of the human mind and spirit, and how they relate to the body and other material phenomena. The issue concerns the relationship between our senses and the reality of the world: do we perceive reality, or is what we perceive an illusion like our dreams? Some philosophers like Plato conjectured a greater reality behind the specific material ones (i.e., Plato's Forms), while Descartes happily decided that the act of thinking and doubting gave proof of his own existence and ultimately that of others as well. Kant combined these approaches by postulating that the human mind perceives things in terms of pre-conceived categories. While philosophy has explored this matter in depth, both science (i.e., psychology) and parascience (e.g., spiritualism, psychic beliefs) also delve into the mind-body problem. In theoretical psychology, Jung's archetypes of individual and cultural experience are comparable to Kant's categories, while parascience posits a parallel spiritual world that is not material but interacts with the one that is.

No matter what type of human inquiry is involved, life still presents a plethora of mysteries. But we may ask, what if we understood it all; would it make life more meaningful and livable, or would it be terminally tedious as a result? This is strictly unanswerable, because it depends on knowing what we do not know now. Certainly, one of the greatest mysteries is the existence of the universe itself, including what may have caused it and our purpose in being alive. Religion and personal beliefs attempt to answer these, and lack of confidence in an answer can cause individuals to have existential crises and despair.

If we knew how and why it all began and our role in it, the answers might provide comfort and greater meaning – or terror and greater despair.

Another angle on this question is that, for good or for ill, the current level of human cognition allows only a small percentage of the population to understand the more complex aspects of life, whether scientific or philosophical. Most of us have only a vague, extremely partial knowledge of biology, biochemistry, physics, philosophy, the arts, technology, etc. Hence, even if everything in life were ultimately "understood" collectively by humanity, the vast majority of humans would remain in a state of vague fascination at life's wonders. Moreover, even those who penetrate life's mysteries often remain fascinated by the answers, as Einstein iconically displayed. So there is little worry about terminal tedium or a kind of "intellectual death" of the universe.

In sum, life in our universe is full of mysteries because it is magical, and it remains so even when we figure out how and why some things work and what goes on inside ourselves. The nature of matter, the existence of life, the formation and evolution of the universe and species, the existence of love and the capacity to care for others, the technological inventions of humans – these and so many other phenomena provide us with an endless array of fascinating subjects to understand. And, when we do, we are usually left with a profound sense of awe and wonder. Propelled by our innate curiosity, we then move to the next wonder of the world and try to uncover the magic within.

Telling Time

WHAT IS IT ABOUT time that it is both mundane, measuring our everyday lives from the start, and mysterious, belying any true definition?

From birth we are time-dated and time-indentured. Although only astrologers care about the exact minute it happens, the date of birth becomes a central fact of our existence as the clock starts ticking on our finite lives. Early on things pass in a near continuum, modulated by sleeping and feeding and occasional candles on cakes with balloons and friends. But soon we become subject to the clock in more discrete ways, like the calls to dinner and bedtime. In adolescence we are expected to observe the clock and adhere to its strictures, getting to school on time and moving from class to class on a finely partitioned schedule ruled by the bell. By adulthood we are full disciples of time, carrying it on our wrist or in our pockets to direct our daily moves, though some are more faithful to it than others.

While our lives are measured in such ways by time, our own perception of it can vary as we age. Conventional wisdom holds that as people get older they feel time pass more quickly. Certainly, adults in career paths and family-rearing have little spare time, and this tends to quicken the apparent pace of time. People at advanced age may feel each day hastens them to their end. But childhood can also pass quickly for youth as well as parent, while seniors without productive lives may feel time passes ponderously. The rationale that time seems faster as one ages because each unit is a smaller part of one's life seems contrived. More likely, it is the quality of one's life at any point that influences one's perception of time, with busier and happier periods feeling more fluid than those where our lives are adrift.

Each individual as well as each culture also seem to have their own sense of time. In a work setting we easily identify those who observe time commitments and those who seem incapable or uninterested in doing so. Some get caught up in their work and "lose track" of time. Others care little about how time passes and its effect on their activities or interactions. So, too, some cultures are known to be punctilious about time, observing it constantly if not religiously, while others have a more casual attitude about the role of time in daily life. This cultural difference became a real issue when the European countries came together in the European Union, as the southern states, with their more relaxed attitude toward time, had to trim it somewhat to keep up with the north.

While time may pass subjectively at different rates, we generally think of it as an objective measure we can rely on. We have clocks and watches that are indifferent to culture or life's vicissitudes. Nowadays our digital toys are endowed with direct connections to satellite positioning systems with very accurate chronometers that are more than sufficient timekeepers for our everyday lives. On the scientific front atomic clocks keep time within extraordinary ranges of accuracy, such as one second in millions of years. Whether it is the ticking of gears or crystals, the swing of the pendulum, or the cycles of radiation from changing atomic states, time appears immutably constant from one measured interval to another. It is just a matter of how accurately and precisely we can measure it.

In almost all situations, this notion that time is constant is a valid one. As children of the age of relativity, however, we know that at very high speeds time behaves elastically, no longer as a fixed constant, depending on the velocity of the system compared to the speed of light. As the system approaches the latter speed, time elongates and seems to slow down. Hence, Einstein's "twin paradox," wherein a twin who leaves Earth in a rocket ship traveling at high speed would return years later younger than his brother. This time "dilation," as it is called, actually occurs at a much smaller scale even at earthly un-warp speeds, but highly precise measurements are needed to discern it.

So time is, for everyday purposes, a constant measure that keeps happening. We can't stop it or, under normal circumstances, slow it down. Deadlines and upcoming events about which we are apprehensive come upon us steadily, while our subjective perception makes them seem to accelerate toward us. People highly sensitive to time feel its inexorable movement and hasten to fulfill their goals in living. Time is like a train or conveyor belt that will not slow down or stop for us no matter what we wish.

What is peculiar about all this is the unidirectionality of time: it always goes forward. We of the film and video age are accustomed to running events backwards to see them at an earlier stage or rerun the action. Not so in real life. Scientists tell us that we would have to travel at a speed greater than light, which is impossible. I suppose this means we would have to "catch up" to the light rays emitted from past events and get there before they were emitted, which sounds daunting indeed. But does this imply that those events are still "out there" somewhere and retrievable, the way we can harvest radiation and events of long ago from other parts of the universe? Are all past events in some sense still extant, every moment of history etched permanently in the cosmos and relivable if we only knew the catalog number?

For something so important to our lives, we know little about what time is or how to describe it. Time is completely immaterial and abstract, and all measures of it are simply mechanisms or events that are steady and regular. We "tell time" by observing moving hands or changing digits on a clock, but these are no more "time" than the word that names it. Our dictionaries, usually so precise in definition, lamely describe time as a sequence of events or a "continuous duration" in which events succeed one another. Does something need to happen for time to exist? A thought experiment suggests not (although there may be no known scenario where nothing happens). And defining time as a duration is, of course, a tautology. Should we conclude that time, like numbers, is an abstraction that humans have invented but does not otherwise exist?

According to current thinking in cosmology, time may indeed not have existed prior to our universe, nor space either. Both space and time were created in the Big Bang, although in the initial moments (the "inflationary" period) these dimensions were nothing like what we now perceive. What may have existed before is not known. Hypotheses range wildly from nothing at all to multiverses to a universe that oscillates between expansion and infinite contraction. In any case, time seems to be quite malleable in the cosmos, unlike our concept of it on Earth.

In some way, time – whatever it actually is or represents – may be a key to the universe and its secrets. It may represent not an external measure of what happens when, but a central force in determining events and what exists in what order. Only in periods of relative calm between cosmic events, such as the current expansionary universe, might time appear to be the uniform "fourth" dimension, a kind of adjunct to the other three that keeps historical record of what happens within them. At the singularities of the universe, whether "in time" or "in space" (e.g., a black hole), time may transform into a dynamic matrix of formless matter, energy, and existence until it manifests itself anew.

Back on Earth, time generally seems mundane and even trivial, the way weather is mostly perceived. When we think about time at all, it is more like a driver, inexorably pushing us along in our lives. But our sense of time certainly helps us understand events, and it provides some order to our lives. Contrast this with a baby, who has no sense of time and for whom all events are entwined or apparently random. While this experience may better reflect the true nature of time, it would make grown-up life less meaningful if not incomprehensible. Better that we can measure the passing of the seasons and days, even if we must put up with the hours and minutes.

Honesty and Integrity

WHAT IS IT ABOUT honesty and integrity that makes them so difficult to practice completely? Is it even possible – or advisable – to live a life of honesty and integrity?

Honesty requires that one speak truthfully and behave consistently with one's professed values. Small deviations from these strictures do not constitute dishonesty. But even keeping within reasonable bounds of honesty is challenging. For one, most of us are not precise enough either in our thinking or in our memory to talk accurately about past events or intentions. We may not realize what we say is untruthful, much less intend it to be so, but if the deviation is significant it can come across as dishonest or, more charitably, being loose with the truth. Furthermore, we do not always consider beforehand whether a particular action conforms with what we profess to others. Saying one thing and doing another – the very phrase, common as it is, speaks to the circumstance we have all found ourselves in.

Clearly, there are two factors involved in honesty: intention and actual word or deed. Intention may be the most significant determinant, but it can be belied by words and deeds. If someone keeps telling us what we know is untrue or often acts inconsistently with their statements, we consider the person dishonest and untrustworthy regardless of their intention. Generally, though, intention leads the way and determines whether words and deeds are honest. We consider an honest person as one who strives to be forthright and true; a dishonest person intentionally shades, distorts, or hides the truth to their own advantage.

The problem is that all of us at some time intentionally shade, distort, or hide the truth. Does that mean we are all dishonest? Complete honesty in one's life is virtually impossible for several reasons. There are inevitable inconsistencies caused by the complexity of daily living and how we process it. There are social pressures to perform or be perceived a certain way that cause us to shade the truth favorably to ourselves. And there are situations where being honest can hurt someone else or ourselves unnecessarily – the "white lie," which is intentionally telling an untruth, usually not very significant, in order to spare someone's feelings. If white lies and shading the truth are allowed in an honest person, how many are acceptable over time? We may be surprised how often we do these.

More seriously, virtually all of us have gone beyond shading the truth or telling white lies on one occasion or another. Perhaps we do not speak outright lies – such as claiming a positive when the negative is true – but rather prevaricate to confuse the issue and suggest something more acceptable. As difficult as being honest is, it has the great advantage of not enmeshing a person in a web of additional lies to protect the initial one. Invariably this happens when a person lies: one untruth must be followed by another because the facts do not support the first, and the lies typically get more convoluted and unbelievable. When the truth inevitably comes out, the person looks much worse than if the truth had initially been confessed.

Of course, telling the truth may not be rewarded and may in fact have painful consequences. Punishment may follow, or a break in a relationship, or worse. People lie to avoid such consequences, and they may succeed, paving the way for future lies. In some cases the truth may not be believed, such as when one is innocent of a transgression but implicated in it. Then one has the worst of both: being honest and still being considered a liar. Honesty may not always "pay" in terms of outcomes, but it surely puts the conscience more at peace.

Honesty also factors highly in the integrity of a person. Integrity encompasses more than being honest, but the latter is a requisite. For integrity involves living a life that is whole, where the parts all align and are not in conflict such as when untruths and deception permeate a person. Integrity means living consistently with high moral standards and decency and not compromising on one's essential values. We consider a person of integrity to be honest and ethical in their dealings, considerate and well-behaved toward others, motivated to contribute to the world, and a model to all. Such a person has an aura of strength and inner calm even if they are driven by a sense of mission.

But avoiding internal inconsistencies and not compromising one's values are difficult. Life presents many gray situations where being consistent with past statements and actions cannot always be achieved. Circumstances may have changed or there may be additional considerations that compel us to respond differently. As a result, we may feel the strain inside as well as the disapproval of critics all too eager to point out the inconsistency. Furthermore, we must sometimes make compromises in our work or at home that may not be entirely consistent with our values. We cannot do something completely at odds with our values and maintain our integrity, but we may still find ourselves not entirely comfortable with the result.

Such realities make integrity a challenge but not unattainable. Key in maintaining integrity is to keep constant check that one's actions and motivations always align with just, humane, and reasonable goals. No compromise or inconsistency should be allowed to violate one's central values; one must also ensure that small deviations don't chip away at the fundamental core. This may put the person at odds with the wishes of the majority, and courage is usually needed to maintain integrity. But others will usually respect the person for it.

Fundamental to integrity is that it have a moral basis. By aligning always with righteous goals, a person of integrity can guard against the trap that befalls many decent people of doing questionable deeds to achieve well-intentioned ends. This phenomenon, more common than we might suppose, is popularly known as the end justifying the means. It isn't surprising in our complicated, compromised world that this happens, with good people having to rationalize certain actions to put them in a better light. But the constant moral compass of integrity can virtually eliminate this practice, which is also a slippery slope to more frequent questionable acts. The moral imperative drawing a line at unsavory means can force a creative search for better ways to achieve just ends. If there is really no alternative, the person of integrity will own up to it and explain honestly why an action was taken.

It is possible, then, to live a life of honesty and integrity, despite the inevitable pitfalls. An unwavering intention to abide by the truth and to pursue just goals qualifies as such a life. No human being can avoid occasional slips of honesty, but one's overall deportment should consist of truthful speech and deeds consistent with beliefs. Moreover, the person of integrity ensures that actions align to the greatest extent possible with moral ends.

But is it advisable in this gritty world to be an honest person with integrity? Is one considered naïve or, worse, a fool in being so? Among most decent and generally honest people, there is a level at which deviations in honesty and integrity are not only tolerated but expected of a sensible person. Most people, for example, would let pass small omissions from their taxes, and some deliberately evade taxes owed on minor matters. These transgressions are justified as actions everyone else takes and, in a personal ethics equation, offsets of what the government gets from us unfairly. How many people, when noticing a non-trivial omission on their restaurant, shopping, or service bill, bring attention to it to rectify it? Surely most will do so in the reverse to eliminate an unfair or excessive charge. But again, one can easily rationalize the omission as compensation for some other way the retailer overcharged.

Despite its professed endorsement of honesty and integrity, Western culture has not always viewed favorably a person with these traits. Our literature has sometimes branded such a person as a simpleton, fool, or idiot. The medieval legend of Parzival or Parsifal concerns an innocent, naïve person, who, in the German version adopted by Wagner for his opera, happens into a lot of trouble before he becomes a hero. Dostoyevsky's novel, *The Idiot*, was a self-proclaimed experiment in how a completely righteous man might fare in contemporary society; the results were not particularly good for him or for others.

While these characters portray extremes of pure honesty and integrity, which none but saints could emulate, a more realistic commitment to honesty and integrity does not need to sow misfortune. Those we consider true leaders in the workplace or social world have found a way to navigate through the temptations and complexities of life and still maintain their honesty and integrity. Every little lie, evasion, or omission can have the effect of chipping away at our soul. Better to be considered a bit naïve than to constantly rewrite one's moral equation to accommodate the exceptions.

Evil

WHAT IS IT ABOUT evil that compels a small minority of humans to pursue it and fascinates the rest of us who ostensibly don't? What makes evil, which is presumably so bad, alluring in a way that other negative human behaviors are not?

Without getting too philosophical or theological, I will define evil as knowingly promoting personal gain to the serious detriment of others. Evil at its worst revels in the harm it inflicts or has no qualms in doing so. Evil-doers may not, however, consider their actions evil if they are amoral, sociopathic, or deluded, or they may rationalize their actions on behalf of a supposed greater good, such as a nationalistic or political cause. Numerous studies of unmistakably evil people have not identified a central cause or characteristic, while a case has been made that everyone is susceptible to committing or condoning evil under the right combination of fairly commonplace circumstances.

The villain of literature and entertainment may revel in his bad, but most bad guys and gals seem as much driven by a criminal mentality as by the satisfaction it brings. This mentality is allured by those actions that, by their disregard for others' pain, provide the surest path to one's self-interested goals. Criminal minds are often seen as cunning and even brilliant, as they must circumnavigate social mores and laws to accomplish their ends. But, like the rich, who keep loading onto their riches, the evil perpetrator never quite seems satisfied by the gains he obtains, and so the mentality becomes a way of life and often a career.

The criminal mentality and the susceptibility of us all to evil are the impetus for much Western religion, law, and governance, which are all armed to limit if not eliminate evil and criminal behavior. It is no accident that eight out of the Ten Commandments are prohibitions on bad or criminal behavior, such as lying, stealing, or murder. Our laws are catalogues of what people should *not* do in our society, and we have set up familial, institutional, and societal authorities to enforce against such behaviors.

Yet, there is surely a difference between many instances of bad behavior and what we label as evil. Not all law-breakers or criminals would even be considered evil. Behaving badly or "doing wrong" prompts most of us to feel guilty, to atone or ask for forgiveness from those we may have hurt. It does not attain the status of evil simply because we intended to do the wrong thing, or even because we were aware it would hurt others. What makes bad behavior evil is more likely the complacent willingness to inflict harm and the low level of scruples attending it. Nor is evil simply a measure of the magnitude of wrong-doing or hurt inflicted. Certainly, it is difficult to exonerate anyone who is aware he is causing great harm, but branding that as evil depends to some extent on his comfort in doing so.

I said at the beginning that evil is generally an activity of a small minority in society, although there is a latent touch of it in virtually all of us. From our own temptations and lapses in hurting others, we can understand how almost all individuals could be prone to doing some evil at some point in their lives. This does not, however, easily translate into societal evil, where the minority essentially becomes the majority, and the latter is accessory to, enables, or condones evil even if it doesn't directly perpetrate it. We see this in some nations taken over by dictatorships and evil regimes, or in societies whose laws or mores contradict their ostensible principles and religious beliefs (e.g., slavery and segregation in the United States). The majority reaps some benefit by allowing evil to occur, even if it claims not to be involved or very much aware.

Just as we cannot identify the true nature of individual evil, we struggle to understand why whole nations at times embrace it. Nazi Germany is the prevailing symbol of collective evil in the modern era, one which that country and others strive to avoid repeating. Countless analyses of the economic and social conditions that led to the Third Reich still fail to explain the pervasiveness of its evil and the thrall in which it held its citizens. We do know that its leader satisfied unmet needs of many citizens, making them more willing to tolerate and even support the regime, while he also exploited common fears and prejudices. To a similar extent evil movements in other societies play on people's needs and bad feelings, and then bank on their willingness to look the other way or believe in false explanations to justify the benefits they receive from evil actions.

The common awareness that societal evil is not a good thing lends hope to its eventual elimination. Yet, its recurrence, even in the modern (post-Nazi) era, makes one wonder if society will ever get beyond evil, whether it will just continue to repeat and recycle itself. I am of the perennially optimistic – or naïve – temperament, hoping that humans can overcome our vices and collectively progress toward a more humane society. I would like, therefore, to believe that human evil will eventually end or become, like smallpox, confined to small pockets of the world or a moral laboratory. I believe I am not the only one with such dreams: in the millennial period there was talk of a coming "end of history" and of being in a "post-racial" period. Recurring genocide and the 2001 terrorist attacks took care of the former, while blatant prejudice in recent years in the U.S. and elsewhere has eclipsed talk of the latter.

Yet, the progress of modern society, where practices once countenanced such as slavery and segregation are now considered reprehensible, suggests that optimism about our collective ability to avoid evil is not unrealistic. Such social progress – while admittedly debatable in some respects – is not, however, mirrored in eradication of individual evil. Regardless of the trend of crimes such as murders from year to year, the sad fact is that crimes and other indisputably evil behavior by individuals continue and appear to be intractable. We can put limits on the potential evil of society, but not that of a minority of individuals, at least not before-the-fact.

Considering the overall trajectory of human evil, the troubling thought arises that, in some perverse way, we willingly tolerate some level of evil and could eliminate it if we really wanted to. This would make sense if society needed evil to define or compel the good – if laws required actual examples of violations, or children and young adults needed counterexamples to prevent bad behavior. This approach more likely applies to the dynamics of Western religion, which uses evil as a counterexample (e.g., the Ten Commandments) and even a personified force (e.g., Satan) to prevent such behavior in most of us. But it seems unlikely from a social perspective in modern societies, which no longer make a spectacle of punishing evil-doers in public and rely on general education and good upbringing to establish norms of behavior.

How then do we explain our continuing fascination with evil and bad behavior and the destruction that often accompanies them? From fist fights to murders, we are drawn to observe and thrill to patently negative acts. Our television and cinemas feature countless scenes where vehicles, buildings, cities, and landscapes are destroyed, not built or protected. (The "feel-good" programs and movies which feature the opposite are rare exceptions.) While not all negative behavior or catastrophe can be classified as evil, it often accompanies evil and allures us in similar ways.

Three explanations can be offered. We must be alerted to these behaviors and actions because they might affect our survival. The "thrill" may, in fact, be the adrenaline that fuels our fight-or-flight response when we feel threatened. We seek out these experiences through entertainment because modern life does not generally provide them, and we are instinctively conditioned to have these reactions as part of self-preservation. Alternatively, the hidden horrors of modern life force us to make these feelings explicit in objectified, fictional form.

Another explanation is that we are all susceptible to evil, so "partaking" in it vicariously without actually committing it allows us to satisfy the temptation. The evil thoughts that we all have at times but do not put into action can be given life by others, who are solely responsible. We can thrill to a fist fight and be fascinated by a murder because we are doing neither. We won't identify directly with a criminal – that would be too much of an admission – but in fiction we want him to give the good guys a good run. We are horrified when the evil goes beyond the limits of what we subconsciously could imagine doing, such as mass slaughter or gruesome murders. In these cases the horror may outweigh the fascination that is still there underneath. So, too, with accompanying destruction: we can revel in it in fiction, but we grow increasingly uncomfortable with it in reality as it comes closer to home.

Still another explanation is that evil provides some pleasure because we see someone getting a benefit for himself, albeit by doing something taboo. We can identify with and vicariously enjoy the personal gain, while not suffering the consequences or guilt of infringing the rules and harming others ourselves.

And that is why other negative human behaviors, such as bad performances, do not attract us as much. They neither resonate with our survival instincts and alter egos nor provide the vicarious pleasure of personal gain. Evil, which we fortunately keep at bay most of the time, can do all three.

Shame

WHAT IS IT ABOUT shame that makes it such a strong and inhibiting emotion? And should we be ashamed to feel shame or to use it against others?

When I was in my early childhood years (perhaps age 3 or 4), I experienced horrific shame when I was changed in front of my peers of both sexes at a nursery. I cried as they watched me with my pants down. I believe I had wet my pants, prompting the changing, which was conducted incomprehensibly in front of everyone. I suppose I was ashamed both of wetting myself and of being exposed, as I was accustomed to neither at that age.

I could recount later incidents of shame – not of the same kind, of course – over something I had done or said, usually in front of other people. I may not have said or done anything inherently shameful, but the situation made me the object of ridicule. Feeling unjustly treated may not preclude feeling shame, as it is strong enough to override most other emotions. Where the ridicule is warranted, the shame goes even deeper, leading to those purple-blush moments when one wishes to vanish instantly. In private one may also feel shame over a deed showing poor judgment or taste, or an act of malice or bad faith toward someone who didn't deserve it. This private shame may be more deeply distressful and even traumatic, depending on what caused it.

Shame derives its strength not only from being a socially-oriented emotion but also from being primitive. It almost always relates to doing something that society or our peers consider bad. If the disapproval of one person we value disconcerts us, the collective disapproval of many shakes us to the core. That is where the emotion affects us, in the gut or likely in the part of the brain where we feel other primitive emotions such as fight-or-flight. For shame signals to us that our position with our peers may be in jeopardy. We have transgressed in a significant way, and we may ultimately be ostracized from our group. Nothing in primitive society could be more dangerous except fighting with a mammoth.

The feeling of shame is virtually impossible to stop or tamp down. In contrast, embarrassment is more easily controlled and overcome, as it represents awkwardness in a social context which may not entirely be of one's making. Although we may be embarrassed about something we say or do, a simple apology may be enough to relieve the feeling. Not so with shame, whose cause usually transcends such an easy solution. Even a brief, fleeting social incident that causes shame may linger in memory for years.

Shame's strength works to society's advantage in inhibiting much bad behavior. Most people when caught with a misdeed or crime feel shame and express remorse accordingly. Society uses shame to prevent crime by making a public example of perpetrators. In colonial America, public stocks held criminals for viewing and disparagement; today the media is sometimes used for this purpose, with social media unleashing millions of individual shamers, often behaving shamefully themselves. Shaming also enforces conformity to society's norms at the personal and group levels, with children mercilessly using it against their idiosyncratic peers and adults more subtly (and viciously) applying it to friend and foe alike. One of the strongest verbal lashings parents can give children is to tell them they should be ashamed of themselves. Even if a child doesn't initially feel shame over his or her action, this statement will likely elicit some shame, coming from the person most respected or feared.

Private shame, briefly mentioned above, represents an advanced form of the emotion even if it is not explicitly public. The individual feeling it has internalized society's disapproval and showers shame upon him or herself. We can be harder on ourselves than others on us, and private shame can be excruciating. It may not have the immediate intensity of public shame, but it can be even more profound. In extreme cases private shame may lead to self-destruction, as the individual feels that the effects of the offending act can never be overcome and life will be grievously compromised henceforth.

The power of shame and its role in maintaining social conformity depend on people being capable of feeling it. There are, unfortunately, rare individuals who seem immune to shame and do shameful things without feeling the consequences of the emotion. We call such people "shameless," which is somewhat ironic, considering their behavior is usually "shameful." For while they do things the rest of us consider shameful, they somehow detach themselves and feel neither shame nor the opprobrium of others. This detachment allows shameless people to violate legitimate norms of behavior toward other people and society, leading to antisocial behavior and potentially criminal or sociopathic acts. Hardened criminals and dictators provide extreme examples, although we all know of lesser examples in our lives.

It is important to differentiate such shamelessness from thoughtful opposition to an unjust social norm or law, such as racial segregation. In the latter case, the individual also defies society without remorse and may inure him or herself from the significant social derision that ensues. But the justice of the cause precludes feeling shame. The possibility of being ostracized or threatened by society may also be real but is considered an inevitable consequence.

These two cases – antisocial shamelessness and principled resistance to shaming – are exceptions to the pervasive power of shame in society. Given its power, should feeling shame as an adult make us feel more ashamed, and should we be ashamed to use shame against others? In the first case, it is true that a secondary effect of shame in a public setting is feeling ashamed to show it, as a person blushes even more deeply when someone (helpfully) points out they are blushing. Clearly, however, as a powerful, primitive emotion, the expression of shame should not make one feel any more ashamed than what legitimately causes it.

As to shaming others, everyone must realize that shaming is a potent act that can quickly become harmful or hostile. One should be very careful about putting others in a public position of shame: not only may it hurt them, but it may cause them to retaliate or respond unproductively. Moreover, the very exposure that public shame entails can cause lasting emotional damage to a person that outweighs the benefit of the correction sought. It is thus advisable to consider less drastic ways of correcting another's faults or misdeeds, unless shame is the only way to get through to a person and motivate change. Of course, shaming for sport, which is rampant in today's social media, constitutes irresponsible behavior that can cause lives to be destroyed. So, too, using shame in any other way to purposely hurt or defame someone. We should always remember that we could be the next one to feel that broiling, primordial, inescapable feeling we call shame.

Animal Love

WHAT IS IT ABOUT loving animals that many people find easier to do than loving other humans? And how do these loves compare?

I speak here primarily of domestic animals, including so-called companion animals, colloquially known as pets. They are generally not the same as animals found in the wild around us, but rather dogs, cats, exotic birds, horses, fish, and such. Rabbits and sometimes snakes come in this category and may be indigenous. Occasionally an animal in the wild may have this relationship with a person, but it is seldom mutual or even acknowledged by the animal (as the pair of loons on the lake outside hardly recognize my existence, much less my adoration of them).

That people shower love on their animals can easily be observed. The care they take in exercising, feeding, and grooming them may be seen daily in any neighborhood or household. The affection they feel toward them is frequently demonstrated by hugs and pettings and words of endearment, with no inhibition about public displays thereof. The depth of love people feel for their animals is attested by the grief they feel on losing them. For many people, the animal in their home is truly another family member.

Yet, the comparison to family also illustrates some differences between animal and human love. The family bond is extremely strong, so being part of the human family shows just how much the animal is loved. But virtually all family relationships are fraught with some tension and conflict, sometimes in significant amounts, while the relationship to the animal is generally not. Certainly, some members of a family may be closer to the animal than others, and vice versa. But the relationship does not usually manifest itself in arguments (or what is comparable), as commonly occurs between human family members. At most, the animal may protest if it[1] is not getting what it wants, and that need is usually fulfilled by the human or denied and trained away. Personal animosity between an animal and its human companion is unheard of, although it can definitely occur between animals and people outside the family (parrots can harbor such a dislike for years).

In every case except love for a wild animal, the animal has a subordinate status to the human. All companion animals are under the care and supervision of their humans. Dogs acknowledge this status openly in accordance with their genetic disposition to live in packs, as the human takes on the role of the lead or alpha dog. Cats, who act as if they are no one's vassal, usually get their food, water, and medical care from their humans. All other animals live in the house or stable with clear boundaries for their behavior, although they may have an independent personality and express their desires boisterously.

In most cases the subordinate status of animals is elevated by the love and care they receive. The animal may be cared for like a human child, but it is loved like one as well. This explains in part the ease with which we love our companion animals. We do not necessarily want something we love to be subordinate to us, nor feel that something subordinate is necessarily lovable. But the stewardship we provide bonds us to our charge, whom we have brought into our lives

---

[1] The impersonal pronoun is used here and subsequently not in disrespect for animals but in its colloquial usage for them when gender is unknown or not relevant.

willingly. The very act of giving through our care fosters a deeper love for the animal.

And what a love this can be. If love is best characterized by deep affection and selfless devotion toward another, the love of an animal fulfills this standard in spades. Most people with a companion animal adore it, pamper it, spoil it, and take good care of its continuing needs. They speak knowingly about the animal's personality and behavior, but with the affection and tolerance parents show toward their children. In many cases the love is fully reciprocated by the animal, above and beyond any interaction to fulfill the animal's needs. Animals often happily play with their humans, surely a sign of affection and trust. Animals have a way of appealing directly to our hearts and bringing out our best (although they are also, unfortunately, abused by some humans who take out their angers and emotional illnesses on them). It is no wonder that animals are increasingly being used as "therapy" for lonely seniors, war-weary veterans, and convicts in rehabilitation.

Love between humans and animals is almost always less problematic, less complicated, and less demanding than love between humans. A "breakup" between human and animal is extremely rare, as the bond between the two, once formed, stays firm, especially on the animal side. Animals are never explicitly critical of their human partners; one might imagine cats thinking ill of us, but we don't have to hear about it. While animals can be demanding in their need for care, affection, and play, the requests are straightforward and generally easy to satisfy. Sometimes an animal becomes neurotic in its needs, as cockatoos when they scream constantly for company or dogs when they bark incessantly, but behavioral training usually solves or mitigates this problem. In sum, an animal and a human that bond together accept each other in a way that humans in relationships don't ordinarily do. Undoubtedly, this unqualified love is a major reason people find such comfort in their animals.

Admittedly, when love between humans works, it can give value that is unique and additional to animal love, although it can require more effort than the latter. The most obvious difference is the sexual relationship that is possible between humans. At the emotional level, humans can provide a level of understanding toward each other that animals cannot through the medium of a common language and experience. Many animals are certainly capable of sympathetically reading their humans, but a friend or lover can not only sympathize with but also empathetically understand what a person goes through. With this level of understanding, humans can give emotional support at a potentially deeper level than animals. These emotional connections are not automatic, of course, and in most cases they take more effort than the simple bond of love. In fact, the lack of these additional connections is often the reason love between humans fails.

Nevertheless, animal love can be strong and deep, as much as love between humans. Most people have been blessed with the experience of loving and being loved by an animal. It is unforgettable, however much the inevitable loss – because most companion animals last a portion of our lifetimes – pains us to the core. The animal who gave the special call when we entered the house and it knew it was us; the animal who ran or flew to us alone among the group when we entered the room; the animal who let us pet and caress it, all with the special affection not given to others who interact with it; the animal who looked at us with unfailing love in its eyes or pose.

We give our hearts to our animals freely and uninhibitedly, without fear we might get hurt or exposed. *There was Willie, our beloved Cocker Spaniel, older and wiser than us children, who all cried when he was found lying in the road; and Ginger, our wild terrier mutt, my first dog love come of age.*

We take all pains to care for our animals, never asking what they would give us in return. *There was Jacques François (le Quinze), our pedigree poodle, whom I walked conscientiously and who returned the love even as I became aloof in college; there was dear Cinnamon, our affectionate rabbit, who broke my son's heart when we had to let her go; and turtles, fish, canaries, and baby alligators we all cared for, but particularly Mom.*

We laugh with and at our animals, but never with malice, just love. *There were my dear kittens, Jason and Caddy, whose feral mother adopted me to house her litter; they wrestled and played with the yarn ball and stared at ghosts across the room so long it frightened me.*

And we comfort our animals in suffering, just as they come to comfort us. *One afternoon long ago, as I suffered from stomach cramps in the living room, my beloved cockatiel, Cary-Bird, flew over and alighted on the sofa where I lay. He looked down at me, then climbed down to be with me. I knew he knew I was in pain and wanted to comfort me. Years later, as he was dying, I went to comfort him, but too late. I will never get over his loss, nor my inability to help him.*

Genius

WHAT IS IT ABOUT GENIUS that makes it so rare, fascinating, and often repellent? Does genius propel society, or is it largely an aberration? And what does genius mean for the rest of us who aren't?

Genius has long been subject to admired characterization or sardonic caricature. Because it is highly individualistic, genius has not always been viewed positively by the rest of society. The European Romantics of the nineteenth century were perhaps the first to elevate genius to an irreproachable level on the presumption that society inevitably shackles the creative forces of the individual, whom they considered supreme. During other periods before and since, genius has not escaped more negative connotations, ranging from wildness and bohemian disregard for social norms to outright evil and satanic behavior.

In reality, genius, like most behaviors, occupies a more middle course. Genius is more likely identified by the level of energy and accomplishment sustained by an individual over a long period than the unkemptness of his or her hair. We are tempted to describe genius as a laser-like focus that the rest of us cannot attain or sustain, and this is certainly true; but equally, genius can be protean in its accomplishments. We would be less likely, in fact, to call someone a genius just because the person is really accomplished in a very narrow area or task. Mastery, which better describes the latter, gives way to genius when the work attains a level and breadth not realized by predecessors through unparalleled intensity and results. Thus, a genius can appear to be like any of us on the outside, but internally will likely be occupied with ever-evolving accomplishments.

Of course, genius presumes a high level of skill or talent in a field combined with intellect appropriate to the endeavor, but these alone do not suffice to explain genius. Edison's famous remark about invention (99% perspiration, 1% inspiration) certainly cautions against the prevailing image of a genius simply handing down great works from on high without much effort. Even those geniuses who seemed to work effortlessly, like Mozart, Bach, or Schubert in music or Picasso and Pope in art and literature, disciplined themselves to sit down and work out the compositions forming in their minds. In most other cases, geniuses spend a great amount of time working out their achievements, more on the model of Beethoven,Michelangelo, or Einstein, who toiled for years to work out the Theory of General Relativity after the "happiest thought" of his life that spawned it. Nevertheless, no one recognized as a genius managed to achieve what they did simply by hard work and effort; a high level of insight, talent, and intelligence was a precondition to their achievements. In sum, both extraordinary ability and considerable effort must combine to produce what genius accomplishes.

These few examples of geniuses raise an interesting question regarding the degree of similarity or difference among geniuses in different fields, such as art, music, literature, and science. Work habits such as described above represent a common characteristic of most geniuses, along with what defines genius regardless of field. But, more deeply, we must wonder whether the qualities of mind characterized by genius are fundamentally different in, say, an artistic field than in science, a profession, or another field of inquiry (e.g., history). To deny such a difference would be to postulate that all geniuses are fundamentally equivalent, or that a specific genius could act genially in any field. And so we are left with a rather generic definition of genius having similar behaviors in different fields, yet with no explanation for what actually makes genius work in any field.

This paradox is compounded by the rather uneven distribution of geniuses in various fields over history and geography. For example, a plethora of musical geniuses inhabited Europe during the eighteenth and nineteenth centuries, but far fewer are recognized in the twentieth century. Instead, science seems to be the source of most geniuses in the latter century, although there were certainly great scientists in the previous two. Likewise, certain countries are known for great accomplishments in specific fields – Germany for music and science, France for art, the United States for science and technology, and England for literature. Such concentrations of genius in specific fields by period and place suggest that external factors such as culture and milieu may be powerful influences on the expression of genius. But this presupposes a more generic form of genius that can, in fact, be molded to a particular field by external influences.

Alternatively, the true nature of genius and its successful expression may be a combination of both internal and external factors. That is, certain countries and periods may select out those geniuses conducive to the culture and milieu, whereas other forms of genius will not be nurtured and may go unexpressed or be manifest in reduced numbers. Would a Bach born in the twentieth century in America reveal himself as a genius, and, if so, in what field? If genius is truly not transferable as to field or expression, are there not many latent, unfulfilled geniuses throughout history relegated to frustrated lives of modest accomplishment because of where and when they were born?

Genius, then, appears to be a rare power of the mind that exhibits similar traits but is specific to a field of intellectual or artistic endeavor. The very rarity of genius sets it apart from merely being at the top level of accomplishment in any field. Genius operates at another level entirely, in a new dimension that typically redefines the subject area in which it works. This exceptional quality makes genius stand out in society as a kind of aberration, putting significant pressure on the genius socially and intellectually.

As rare and outlying as geniuses are in society, they can nevertheless have an outsized effect on a culture and its historical course. This is particularly clear in the scientific and political realms but occurs in all fields where genius is displayed. After all, genius represents a new beginning in any field, a new perspective or form of expression. For the most part, this quantum leap is beneficial for society by revealing new ways of perceiving, living, or understanding. Any number of examples comes to mind, from Newton and Einstein in science to Michelangelo and Picasso in art to Shakespeare and Faulkner in literature. Those geniuses who are considered to consummate an era rather than forge a new one – such as J.S. Bach in music – nevertheless achieve a much higher level of mastery in the conventions in which they work. Their genius also expresses itself in multiple forms, and they leave behind a substantial legacy unmatched by their predecessors.

One might wonder to what degree genius is necessary to effect change. Would the General Theory of Relativity have been discovered without Einstein? (The Special Theory of Relativity most likely would have been.) Would Nazism have arisen in postwar Germany without the evil genius Hitler? Are the accomplishments of several individuals together sufficient to achieve what one genius does, or does it really require the quantum leap inherent in a singular genius? Of course, since history cannot be conducted experimentally, we can never know the answer to these questions. They may not even be valid inquiries, since any historical development is the result of myriad factors in combination. We can, however, say with certainty that geniuses have significant impact on society and history in far greater ways than most other individuals.

Because they are fundamentally change agents, whether they seek to be or not, geniuses may initially be derided or resisted before their work becomes so compelling that it cannot be denied. Part of the Romantic myth of genius, aside from the bohemian lifestyle, is the lack of acceptance by society, living in poverty, and being unappreciated or undiscovered until it is too late for the genius (who dies young) to benefit. Such a fate has certainly occurred, but it is not necessary nor is it typical. Geniuses vary in their ability to navigate society, while some actually thrive on the attention their genius attracts and help convert it into iconic imagery.

For the rest of society not involved in the fields in which they work, geniuses are considered fascinating if not mythical. After all, genius operates at a level that most people consider beyond any possibility of their attaining. The accomplishments of geniuses, whether understood or not, are sufficient cause for the admiration they receive, while the limited grasp of a genius's work can contribute to a greater sense of awe for them. Added to the work of a genius may be an idiosyncratic persona, which often accompanies such an extraordinary individual and may contribute to their legend. One thinks of Richard Feynman on his bongo drums, Immanuel Kant with his daily walks by which citizens set their watches, and Beethoven's apartment cluttered with dirty dishes he had no time to clean.

Yet, for many geniuses we feel a kind of repulsion as much as fascination. Their persona may contribute to this aversion, especially when the idiosyncracies are antisocial or bizarre. But there is more to it than that. For while we may admire genius, few of us would truly want to be one. The intensity of a genius's life seems to be necessary to produce their extraordinary accomplishments, and living nearly constantly at such a high energy level is not desirable for most people. Moreover, geniuses are typically consumed by their work, and little time is left for more mundane activities most of us engage in outside of work, such as family and recreation. It is almost as if geniuses have to make a Faustian bargain to accomplish their goals that distorts their lives in ways most people would find unacceptable, if not abhorrent.

Consequently, few people regret not being geniuses or reflect poorly on themselves in comparison with them. Geniuses are considered outliers, not part of normal experience, like many phenomena in the universe beyond our secular lives. Although we realize that geniuses have to work hard, too, their special abilities are clearly a "divine" gift they did not earn and we did not forfeit. The uncharitable dictum of composer Richard Strauss that humans can be categorized by those with talent and those without applies as well (if less usefully) to genius, but it makes clear that neither talent nor genius is entirely within an individual's control. We are, however, more likely to envy and yearn for talent, which seems more within reach, than genius. From the latter we can be enlightened beyond our imagination and obtain a new understanding of the world even as we return, contentedly, to our more mundane lives.

Spaghetti versus Linguini

WHAT IS IT ABOUT spaghetti that it delights common-sense people universally, yet linguine is the culinary choice of chefs and snobs?

Spaghetti may be served with plain sauce or meat sauce, with meatballs or sausages, with butter or oil. Linguine must be served with a fancier spread such as clam sauce or mussels, or it seems out of place and, well, just flat.

Spaghetti is always round, linguine always flat. We are told, improbably, that the latter is necessary to hold the sauce. Yet we don't see spaghetti sauce falling off the heap on the plate, and the meatball or sausage seems to stay put pretty well on top of it.

I am a lifelong aficionado of spaghetti, although I occasionally partake of linguine with clams or mussels, primarily because I am supposed to. But flat noodles don't behave the same way as round ones on the plate or in the stomach. All sides are the same with spaghetti, so it intermixes easily and fluidly. Not the same with linguine, which gets all tangled up with the flat side rubbing against the edges of other noodles. Your digestion improves with spaghetti, you can take my word for it.

I am tempted to compare this weighty matter with what faced our ancestors a half-millennium ago, with Flat Earthers versus Round Earthers. Despite growing evidence, many people clung to the erroneous notion that the Earth is completely flat (apparently, there remains a small percentage who still believes this). In like wise, although most all children grow up on spaghetti, whether from a can or a package, when they reach a certain age where being contrary is socially cool, they forsake spaghetti as childish or conventional and make a point of ordering linguine in front of their friends. Flat is in, the more so because they never had linguine as children. Incredibly, some Italian menus don't even offer spaghetti, especially in restaurants with nouvelle Italian cuisine (another sore subject, as the "red-sauce" variety suits me fine).

Yet, as we have seen in other essays in this book, there may be more than initially meets the palate when it comes to the shape of spaghetti versus that of linguine. The difference actually reflects a profound, even critical divide in one's approach to life. I've already asserted that for people with common sense spaghetti is the pasta of choice, while snobs make a point of ordering linguine. This is just the beginning. A more thorough comparison reveals the following personality traits in lovers of each:

Spaghetti	*Linguine*
common sense	snobbish
straightforward	devious
harmonious	recalcitrant
healthy	ailing
civic-mnded	rebellious
amicable	surly
optimistic	pessimistic
moderate	extreme
conventional	aberrant
basic	acidic
casual	studiously informal
happily bottle-fed	denied breast-feeding
well-adjusted	chronic psychotherapy

In short, if you prefer linguini over spaghetti, it's because you never learned to eat your spaghetti properly as a child and, frustrated by its always falling off your fork, you became maladjusted and potentially sociopathic.

That is not all.

In the shape difference there is more cosmic meaning than what pertains to the Earth. Except for ugly objects like asteroids and exploding gases like nebulae, the universe is comprised of generally spherical objects. (We'll ignore the slight ellipsoid shape of the Earth and other rotating objects; we also acknowledge that not all spaghetti strands are perfectly spherical in cross-section.) That the Milky Way appears like a disk is irrelevant because that is an artifact of the conglomeration of objects within it as viewed from afar, not the true shape of any of them. It is, in short, a universe of spheres we exist in.

The originators of spaghetti no doubt had the cosmic view in mind when they fashioned their noble creation. Its round rods or cylinders aptly reflect the universe above Mount Vesuvius, near where it was first made. God only knows what got into the mind of the person who thought to "improve" on it with linguine. Of course, that person hailed from Liguria, near France, where they think they know better about everything (culinary especially), hence the inevitable snobbery associated with linguini right from the beginning.

Moreover, spaghetti has quite modern cosmic applications that linguini does not. The fundamental objects of string theory, which is thought to best describe our combined relativistic and quantum universe, look like spaghetti, not linguini (see diagram from Wikipedia for proof of this claim). The

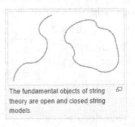

The fundamental objects of string theory are open and closed string models.

spherical approach thus triumphs in the most profound and unbounded way over the flat one. Spaghetti describes a world that, we are told, has ten dimensions, although we can only perceive four (three in space, one in time). Spaghetti even opens us up to manifold universes, if we forgive the contradiction in terms. Linguini, sadly, resides in two dimensions in a single universe.

It is the author's fervent hope that, after perusing this essay, any lingering linguinists will re-consider their ways. As for the author, he must confess at last that, despite his lifelong love of spaghetti, his personality traits more nearly resemble those of linguini. (He has kept this until the end not to distract from the basic truth of his thesis.) He can only surmise that his early complaisance as a child in accepting and then demanding spaghetti in the form of Chef Boyardee in cans warped his taste for spaghetti, and hence his relationship with his fellow humans and with the universe itself. He eats linguine with clam sauce in restaurants as occasional penance.

Family

WHAT IS IT ABOUT family, that it involves such a range of positive and negative emotions and experiences? Is there any realistic alternative to family for human beings?

We may distinguish two kinds of families in a person's life: the family of origin, into which a person is born; and the family a person may form through procreation or adoption. The two kinds share certain characteristics but not all, since in the first a person is the offspring and in the second, an adult. In both cases the family typically lives together for a number of years. But in the first case, one has absolutely no choice who one's other family members are, while in the second case the spouses at least can choose one another. As well, one reacts differently as a child than as an adult to similar stimuli and stresses in a family.

Given the limited choice involved with family members, it is no wonder that personalities can clash and intense conflict result. Having the same parents and similar genes is no guarantee of similar dispositions; it is, in fact, quite common for siblings to be unlike one another. Parents and children can equally be at odds despite their common heredity. Parents may also feel more of a bond with one child or another, although they generally take great care not to show a preference. Even when family members have a close relationship, they can fight endlessly and argue over anything. The very similarity in makeup can breed a "familiarity" that irritates or exasperates one another. Such patterns often persist when the children grow up.

Aside from the psychological complexities, merely living together in close quarters inevitably causes friction. Each individual in a family has their own lifestyle, needs, habits, and preferences. These can involve wake-up time or bed time, levels of noise produced and tolerated, eating habits and tastes, cleanliness and neatness, time in the bathroom, and communication styles, among others. Even if the parents are compatible in all these areas – and there is no assurance they will be – the children may not be compatible with one another or with the parents. Essentially, families put in close proximity two people with general compatibility and any number of offspring who, despite similar genetic makeup, may have different dispositions and habits. It would be a miracle if everyone's behavior aligned day-to-day.

Indeed, these differences and the conflicts they can cause often manifest themselves in families more frequently than love or affection. The rush of daily routines can produce conflict among family members tending to their different needs. So-called family time, such as at dinner, can bring up conflicts relating to lifestyles and responsibilities (such as how and what one eats, who cleans up, etc.). Special family times like holidays can bring out the best and the worst, as people are expected to be together for prolonged periods and to maintain a festive mood. This doesn't always work, of course, as family members can't always act their best and avoid reverting to more typical behavior. In any case, the long time together often requires some relief, whether walking outside or watching television or a movie.

On the positive side, families can create some of the strongest bonds between human beings and lasting love and support. Responsible parents look after their children as long as they live; conscientious children take care of their aging parents as much as they can. Siblings usually stay in touch throughout their lives and help each other in times of need. Some cultures make family the central relationship and any violation of that bond a grievous offense. The genetic or blood bond can override petty irritations and even personality conflicts between family members. We will forgive transgressions of family members more readily than almost anyone else's. In part, we do so because we are tied to our family members, and making a permanent break or being estranged from them is a very serious act with lasting consequences on both sides.

One may fairly ask whether the familial bond is truly love or just a genetic connection. Certainly, the latter figures strongly in family, and it can even come into play between spouses through their mutual genetic connection with their children. Genetic affinity creates a primordial level of attachment among family members that involves a variety of emotions, including love. It may not be a love that always appreciates a family member for the person he or she is, but it is unconditional in being felt regardless of what kind of person the family member is. Why would such love, which can also provide continuing care and support, not be considered true?

Family also refers to those beyond the immediate nuclear unit of parents and children, including grandparents, uncles and aunts, cousins, and in-laws. These relationships may vary in quality, but they are generally not as intense as those in the nuclear family. The one typically closest to the latter is the relationship between grandparent and child, and this is almost always positive or, at worst, neutral. Members of the extended family may or may not live together with the nuclear one, depending on the culture and circumstances (such as financial or health). If they do, some of the same dynamics come into play as with the nuclear family itself. Parental in-laws sometimes live with a family but more often are visitors, delighting the grandchildren and potentially helping with child care.

Family adds an entire dimension to human experience that cannot easily be replaced. On the positive side are love, warmth, companionship, models for behavior, and support provided throughout life; on the negative, friction, disruption, and potentially harmful relationships that can affect a person permanently. Most families have a mix of good and adverse characteristics, and while almost all families have a "skeleton in the closet," most are not fundamentally bad. More typically, there are problems and issues that have to be worked out or managed. The lasting nature of family bonds compels its members to get along to some extent.

For an adult, not having a family can make life simpler and more predictable. Living alone means not having to accommodate others or share space. One may not be able to escape one's family of origin, and relationships and events therein may still affect one's life. But the addition of spouse and children dramatically increases the complexity of life and the circumstances beyond one's control. The gain in simplicity and control by eschewing family comes, however, with the loss of its potential benefits and rewards.

Humans have yet to find a good alternative to the nuclear family. While family can be viewed as a functional unit to produce and raise offspring, it involves much more emotionally and in other ways that fulfill adults and children alike. The communal family, where offspring are not tied to their biological parents and groups of adults take care of the children collectively, was tried in some counterculture communes of the 1960s and 70s. But collective responsibility does not make for very intimate bonds between adult and child, nor can most adults comfortably relinquish their children (or mates) to others. Having no families at all – raising children anonymously with respect to their parents by adults performing this service, as in an orphanage – has all the horror of such an institution. (The orphanage across the street from the house where I was born was a big forbidding building with extensive grounds all fenced around. When a small private airplane crashed into the building, it seemed like a dagger in an already wounded heart.)

Family relationships in some respects replicate those in society at large. There are authority figures (parents) who generally run the show and subordinate coevals (siblings) who may cooperate or compete with one another. Alliances may form at each level and between levels. Favor and affection may be sought between parent and child and in either direction. Typically, children close in age compete with one another for parental attention and with respect to their performance, just like people in a work setting. Sibling rivalry usually abates in adulthood but may linger in some form throughout life. Although the world doesn't really care whether one sibling outperforms another, it is probably an atavistic reaction that cannot be helped. No doubt in primitive times, when humans had fewer resources readily available, siblings did have to compete for food and care, as they do to this day in many animal species.

It is often said that contemporary society works against family and tends to pull it apart. The rise in divorce rates over the last century, now around fifty percent, certainly contributes to this tendency. But there are other forces today that also strain the family bond.

Increased mobility separates parents and children from the time the latter grow up. Increased urbanization puts children in touch with many more peers. Increased wealth allows children to immerse themselves in entertainment and avoid conventional household chores. Increased education provides offspring with many options for their own careers different from their parents. And today's social media connections provide everyone with ample ways to relate to people outside the family. Respect for authority always seems to diminish with each modern generation, but it more likely just remains lower than in more traditional times. Family bonds can remain strong, but there are many centrifugal forces that also pull at family members.

Overall, family may be the worst form of social and procreative unit – except for all the others. Nothing else provides the close bond between parent and child or continuing mutual support for people throughout their lifetimes. Tensions and conflicts in family interactions are part of the human experience. Whether the worst aspects like abuse, incest, and domestic violence can be eliminated through education, awareness campaigns, or individual therapy remains an open question. If they can, family can approach the ideal it is often made out to be.

Prayer

WHAT IS IT ABOUT prayer, that I do it despite being agnostic?

Here are some possible reasons: 1) I am hedging my bets; 2) I am conditioned to pray; 3) I need to appeal to something; 4) I am desperate; 5) I am fascinated by rituals; 6) I am getting old. Let's look at each of these reasons in turn.

Being agnostic is itself one of the great hedges in life. One is not denying the possible existence of God or a greater power, just falling back on one's ignorance about the matter. To pray is to reach out to a possible power that would be greater than myself and may have control over events that I (or other humans) do not have. I do so hoping that power will not mind if I am not sure it exists, at least in a form that might be responsive to my entreaty.

Prayer in this context is a hedge, and one could say I am "hedging my bets" by not fully believing but still asking for favors from God. Others of a more religious bent might call this hypocrisy or even blasphemy, but I prefer the forgiving version of God, not the jealous one (if there is one). This use of prayer has been reported to be a deathbed response by a few agnostics and atheists, most famously, perhaps, the "Great Agnostic," Robert Green Ingersoll, an American lawyer and politician of the nineteenth century. He is reputed to have gasped for the last time, "O God, if there be a God, save my soul, if I have a soul!" Unfortunately, no one knows how this was received (if it was received).

Another possible reason I pray is that prayer is promoted and commonplace in our Western culture, so I am accustomed to it and take it as a natural means to wish for good outcomes. All Western sects appear to use prayer in some form. Outside formal religion, those of a certain age grew up with prayer in school as well as grace at the dinner table. Moments of silence, typically meaning silent prayer, are also common in many public ceremonies. We are conditioned that when hoping for the future and for good fortune of an appropriate kind, prayer is used when it is largely out of our power to ensure the results.

This reason seems plausible but also begs the question. For we are "conditioned" to do a lot of things by society but don't voluntarily do them. Many people grow up going frequently to a house of worship, but they don't do so when they become independent and leave the natal home. We may be exposed to a certain belief – political, social, or religious – but choose subsequently to forge our own. Why would prayer be different, especially for an agnostic?

Perhaps prayer occurs because of the need to appeal to *something* when wishing for the future. Merely hoping for good outcomes doesn't seem sufficient. In the face of the vast emptiness of the universe and the general indifference of society, a direct appeal to a possible higher power gives comfort that neither emptiness nor indifference can bring. It does presume that something out there is listening to us and will respond, if we get the prayer right. So belief plays a role here more than conditioning, otherwise it is merely a mechanical exercise, as it seems to be for some people.

In other words, in this view prayer is a way to fortify a hope by tying it to a causal agent that can actually provide for it. It may seem foolish to send out a wish to the cosmos on the slender belief that it will be heeded – something like a rescue note in the proverbial bottle set to sea – but the act of prayer thereby elevates an internal wish to a potentially cosmic concern. It does, necessarily, presume some level of belief that there is a God to appeal to for one's wish. But it makes prayer more meaningful because of the linkage to something outside that could actually effectuate the wish.

A little background might be helpful about my use of prayer. I never prayed when younger unless prompted to do so. My voluntary prayer only began some twenty years ago when our son had a serious illness. This is admittedly the classic case of turning to religion – or divinity – when desperately in need. I have continued a daily prayer to this day, and the prayer has expanded to cover others in need as well as to maintain the health and welfare of family, friends, and the world.

Praying only as a last recourse or when conditions get bad certainly demonstrates a theological weakness by Western standards. We are expected to have continuing belief in God, not a relationship of convenience or personal necessity. The latter is seen as self-serving and therefore contrary to true devotion to God. Indeed, those who turn to prayer in "time of need" often forget about it (and the divinity they supplicated) when the crisis has passed.

Prayer to alleviate desperate conditions aligns closely with the first, hedging bets. We are content to go our own way as long as things go right. When they go awry, we anxiously ask for help from a power we hitherto ignored. This is similar behavior to the deathbed conversion of agnostics and atheists. But it is entirely natural considering the way most of us live our secular lives. Day-to-day concerns, occupations, and family fill our time and attention. When life goes along reasonably smoothly, we might pause occasionally to appreciate our good fortune; but most of us continue forward to the next task or matter. Only when life is seriously disrupted in crisis do we typically appeal to the divine to intercede.

Praying only when in need may not fulfill most religious tenets, which call for constant faith in the divine and devotion beyond personal need. But it is certainly better than praying for every little thing in one's life or mental shopping cart. People are entitled to believe what they want and to have their own religious rituals. Yet, I find it offensive when someone makes a public display of their religion that trivializes it, such as professional baseball players who thank heaven as they round the bases after a routine home run. God may be involved in everything, but it is rather narcissistic to think God cares about every hit one makes.

Speaking of rituals, since I began the personal prayer mentioned above, I have noticed how it has evolved over time, in terms of both the wording and the gestures I make while saying it daily. This has led me to understand better how prayer rituals (and rituals in general) develop. All religions are full of rituals, many of which seem puzzling at best, ludicrous at worst. In this view, I pray because I am fascinated by how my prayer becomes ritualized and how its rituals change. I don't think this is a motivating reason, but the fascination is genuine.

Two additional questions follow, however: why do rituals emerge and accompany prayers? and why do the rituals change over time? A few examples from my prayer might help explain.

I begin the prayer pleading for the safety, health, and welfare of my children. As I name each, I throw out oral kisses in their direction (wherever they currently are with respect to me) and look at the top of a (preferably evergreen) tree. The words certainly preceded these two gestures. The first (kisses) is a way to connect lovingly, if remotely, with them. The tree represents life (there is, indeed, a tree of life in many religions and mythologies), which I wish to endow them with. These ritual accompaniments connect the words in the first case to the subjects, and in the second, to the wished-for state itself. Like the third reason for prayer given initially, the rituals give the words additional meaning and potential causal relation, rather than simply being stated. I don't recall when I began either ritual, or if they came together (as they do in this *ex post facto* exegesis). But I clearly felt the need for something more than the mere verbal wish.

Additional rituals may follow for similar reasons, or to connect with other non-prayer rituals one might have in one's life. For instance, I conclude my prayer by knocking on wood – preferably a living tree, evergreen first choice – ten times. I knock on wood occasionally for other wishes, usually for people's health. I do it ten times in case I forget to do the prayer on some day. Neither makes much sense except in wish-logic, based on other themes such as the tree of life. At some point I do recall having to stop adding rituals to the prayer, as it became burdensome, distracting, and, well, possibly ridiculous to look at (I generally do it outdoors when I can).

Changes to given rituals may occur to improve or make more precise the intention. As a small example, in the opening where I look at the top of a tree, where there are multiple evergreens, I may look at a whole circle of them to give added weight to the life theme. This is like having a string of rosary beads to multiply the benefit derived from just one prayer (or bead).

Admittedly, I don't conduct my daily prayer simply to enact or analyze rituals; I really do wish for what I pray for. So, we come to the last possible reason why I am doing this as an agnostic, which is that I am getting old. We'll ignore the fact that I began the prayer not quite that old; nonetheless, is it just another manifestation in the aging process of a hedge, or a mental and spiritual weakness that surrenders to a *deus ex machina* to accomplish what I cannot do myself?

It may be true that older people are more likely to turn to prayer than youth. Is this from weakness or, rather, greater experience of the vicissitudes of life and the limitations of humans to control them? After all, young people tend to think of themselves as invincible (research has shown), and when everything is working physically they feel they are completely in control of themselves. Only with age and infirmities do we realize how little we control even the basic biological processes within us (although we can, of course, influence them for good or ill). Similarly, experience teaches most wise people that there is little they can actually control in life, that shaping events and managing one's own actions are the best one can usually do. Prayer is a natural response to this realization, invoking a higher authority beyond one's span of control.

In summary, I pray for all these reasons. I hope my prayers are heeded by whatever is there. I repeat them every day because that is a ritual I am accustomed to. I pray because there is so much at stake, with my children and all the children of the world and its species. I pray because, while I do not know, I do hope.

The Learning Arc

WHAT IS IT ABOUT learning a task that we get the knack just when it is finished and we don't have to do it again?

I am not particularly handy, unlike my father, who was plumber, tinkerer, mechanic, and fix-it-all when he wasn't caring for his patients. So perhaps this matter pertains only to those of us who are challenged when faced with a practical physical problem, such as replacing a door knob assembly. I must first figure out what needs to be done, then how to do it. Even with directions or advice, I typically require several trials to implement the solution. With repetitive tasks I improve over time, as each instance teaches me better how to do the task right. But if there is any interval between these iterations, I have to start over and re-learn what to do. Similarly, once a task is completed, I forget later how to do it unless I have written detailed instructions for myself, which is the last thing I want to do after the work is done.

Now, this heuristic issue is certainly not confined to the physical world. Many abstract problems prove challenging in the same way, particularly for people not adept at them. For instance, mathematics problems must generally be practiced repeatedly to solve them, and after a while most of us forget how to do them. The academic cycle accommodates this lapse by giving students a short span of time (typically, a semester) in which to remember the material, after which (having passed the exam) they may forget it. Only when they must use the learning in a subsequent course do students have to go back and re-learn what they forgot.

Of course, where a mental or physical skill is used constantly, as in an occupation or avocation, the knowledge to perform a task is maintained at a proficient level. It may improve steadily even so, but the difference over time involves refining a skill, not learning or re-learning it. Metaphorically, the learning arc flattens and continues slightly upward, perhaps reaching an asymptote at some point when nothing more can be improved with a given method. When a new approach is discovered that makes a task easier or more effective, this flatter arc is broken through and a new one cuts above it. Depending on the complexity of the newer approach, it may take practitioners time to learn it and the curve may initially be steep.

The problem of the learning arc is thus primarily one for an amateur, especially a beginner. Experienced amateurs and professionals typically go through the arc once and don't have to repeat it unless they have to learn a new skill or a new way of doing something. What we buy from a professional is the assurance that they have a level of proficiency to accomplish a task successfully, without hesitation or undue error, because they are at the top of the curve.

What frustrates me as a rank amateur in most practical tasks is that the learning part of the arc seems to correspond to the duration of the task. Even where the work appears to be straightforward, some complication arises that must be solved. After such a work-around I proceed through the next steps until another complication rears up. Each challenge forces some learning that must be retained for the next unit of similar work. Oddly but inevitably, this process continues until the task is nearly finished, at which point I have attained proficiency and confidence to perform the task well – but there is no more task to do.

Several explanations can be offered for this phenomenon. Just as one fills up the time allotted to do a task, so might we subconsciously give ourselves time to learn it until the end? Using all the time available may be a form of procrastination, if not indolence. If the steps ahead seem endless and repetitive, we have time to learn them as we go. This puts less pressure on us, allowing us to get up to speed slowly and surely. From another angle this might seem counterproductive by increasing the amount of work required before attaining proficiency, but the tradeoff spares us from having to learn everything all at the beginning. In essence, the longer learning arc provides some relief from a task we may not enjoy by spreading out the effort.

Another explanation follows from the first. If we are not naturally suited to the task, we probably have an underlying psychological resistance toward learning how to do it. This is a common problem experienced in many subject areas. I spoke at the beginning about getting "the knack" of a task; for an amateur, the lack of the knack constitutes a real impediment to learning. It means that our functional channels are not aligned with the task, and our learning channels have not yet oriented to accomplish this. When the latter does occur and we begin to feel the natural flow of a task, our attitude changes and we enjoy it more. But this process takes time to overcome the innate resistance, and the more work that lies ahead, the more resistance we may have. That may be why "the knack" occurs toward the end, however paradoxical that may be.

Finally – with apologies to the more rational among us – the delay in learning until the end may be explained as just another instance of the perversity of life. Admittedly, this may be an ersatz explanation, but it is striking how often the phenomenon occurs, making things harder for those least able. As if by malevolent design, we attain mastery just in time to pack it up. Visions of continuing the task effortlessly like a professional haunt us for days afterward, with no outlet for the newly won expertise. Then we forget about it, and indeed, when the task comes up again, we have forgotten how to do it. Could one conjure a more perverse scenario?

Well, yes, on a grander scale even. For in many ways this kind of arc fits the scale of learning over a person's lifetime, in which one gains a kind of competence only in the later years. Living involves so many learnings related to dealing with other people, navigating human institutions, and, most of all, managing oneself and one's own life course. Yet, so many of these life skills seem garnered over time and most skillfully applied later in life – nearer the end, not the beginning, of the task of living. The cumulative learning peaks as we get older, just when both career and society begin to pass us by. We look back and wonder at some of the decisions we made when younger, knowing there is no second chance. For unlike the simple tasks described above, there is no coming back later to the task at this scale.

But perhaps this takes an overly pessimistic view of the learning arc of life. Although each life must be lived individually, it does not have to be experienced separately. Just as friends help each other through crises, the older and wiser can help the younger boost their arc so as not to repeat the same mistakes. In fact, advice is readily proffered by the older to the younger, and occasionally the latter do take note of it. Conversely, the energy and enthusiasm of youth can rekindle interest and experimentation in older people, affording them the opportunity to try something new (or re-do something old) and to use their hard-earned wisdom to shorten the learning arc on the next challenge. Only where resignation sets in, whether in young or in old, do life skills become dormant and the learning arc descends. For learning is truly lifelong and a sign of being alive to the world around us – even if it takes a while to get the knack of it.

Music

WHAT IS IT ABOUT music that appeals universally, yet does so in many different forms and styles? Is our civilization a special incubator for music creation, and could we imagine our world without music?

Much has no doubt been written about music's appeal, with psychologists and physiologists weighing in. This essay does not attempt to reiterate these findings, as the questions raised here go beyond the possible correlation between rhythm and heartbeat. My concern is rather with the significant role music appears to play in our lives, despite – or because of – the wide range of musical expression in our culture.

Consider how many ways we hear or listen to music every day. Ubiquitous are the jingles from television, radio, and now the Internet accompanying commercials and programs. We get bombarded with melodies in many retail stores and restaurants, in building elevators, and even in doctors' offices. Many people now spend a large portion of their time hooked up to a device that plays their favorite music, whether they are jogging, walking the dog, or working. And for live music we can go to concerts, nightclubs, or many a city street corner. Sometimes we hear music we would rather not, such as a neighbor's loud stereo or the pieces meant to appease us on interminable telephone holds.

The range of forms and styles in this musical offering is staggering. They vary in complexity from ditties sung in commercials and nurseries to symphonies played by a hundred instruments. There are formal and informal styles, vernacular and esoteric formats, and untold combinations of voice and instruments.

Western music is broadly divided into popular, classical, rock, and jazz, and each of these genres has its own array of forms and styles. To someone steeped in one genre, the musical language, terminology, and forms and styles of another genre can be like a foreign language. Typically, each person develops a preference for one genre or another, and for certain forms and styles of music in the chosen genre. These preferences might seem to correlate with personality and temperament, such as classical music being associated with formal and reserved types, popular with casual and extroverted, and so on. But looking at the actual followers and practitioners in these genres contradicts such generalities, as all types of people show interest in each of the genres. This makes it even harder to understand why most people cannot bridge the genres and deeply appreciate more than one. A glance at someone's library of recordings usually reveals the predominance of one genre.

Professional musicians, too, operate almost exclusively in one genre; the few who "cross over," such as between classical and jazz or popular, are notable exceptions.

For some people, what passes as music in a different genre may be so alien to their tastes that they would argue it is not music. This was certainly the reaction of many older people in the mid-twentieth century to the advent of rock music, and likely how some felt when jazz emerged earlier in the century. So we should not be too surprised about the inability of most people to genuinely appreciate more than one genre of music. What one becomes accustomed to listening to and enjoying becomes the norm, and significant variations from it are difficult for most to accommodate. How these norms become established in a given individual, however, remains an open question: what makes a particular genre appeal to someone in the first place? I know in my case it changed rather suddenly in early adolescence, as my early exposure to classical did not take hold until I tired one summer of the ever-changing "hit parade" of popular music and wanted something more enduring.

Second-level preferences, involving forms and styles within a genre, can be almost as strong and individualistic. Some rock fans like hard rock, others soft rock; some jazz followers the blues, others bepop or swing; while classical music lovers often divide between opera lovers and opera avoiders. These varying tastes make sense because the subgenre forms and styles can be significantly different from each other. "Schools" may be formed around a particular style of music, and debates and arguments can break out between followers of different schools. This seems to happen amicably in jazz or pop. The staid classical music world, in contrast, has had some vicious battles among various schools, especially when a revolutionary new style emerged suddenly, such as the "new German music" in the mid-nineteenth century (Wagner, Liszt, and such) or atonal music (Schoenberg et al.) in the early twentieth century. One can be amused in retrospect by reports of riots breaking out at the premier of Stravinsky's *Rite of Spring*, but the people there obviously felt strongly that this music was either outrageous or seminal.

At the risk of being obvious, we may ask why there are so many different genres, forms, and styles and what this variety relates to. Much of it evolved historically and to some extent geographically, especially in older times when communication was far less global. Folk and indigenous music provide examples, along with national styles in major genres like classical. Jazz itself most likely developed in New Orleans, but quickly spread to a number of other American cities. With its African-American roots, it sounds distinctly different from, say, Irish music. Each culture "cultivated" its particular sounds over many years, just as plants and animals develop differently, depending on region.

The forms and styles within genres change over time, too, just as so many other cultural characteristics evolve as new generations refresh their view of the world through art. A salient example comes from classical music in its evolution from Baroque to Classical and then to Romantic and Post-Romantic styles. Of course, these groupings become more apparent in retrospect and rarely occur with a clear division over time or style. Some composers bridged the styles or exemplified the transition in their own work. Elements of previous styles remain in the foundation of succeeding ones. Attempts to define the styles also frequently falter as they become victim to over-simplification and false categorization. But changes in style are real and audible, certainly at intervals of half-centuries.

The paradox looming above all this variability is the appeal of music in some form to nearly everyone. What holds all this together to give such universal satisfaction? We know it cannot merely be sounds or the stimulation of our auditory nerves; random sounds are "noise," not something we would tune in to hear (and only considered music in the aleatory movement of the twentieth century). Though most Western music shares the components of melody, harmony, and rhythm along with adherence to the diatonic scale, the sheer variety of combinations of these components – which makes music continually original and interesting – does not guarantee satisfaction in every manifestation. Yet, enough comes together in nearly every genre, form, and style to please significant numbers of people.

Perhaps the differences we feel so strongly among the genres, forms, and styles are, at a larger scale, less significant because the similarities are much greater. These common elements include sounds that work together, a rhythmic flow, and some shape to the sounds and flow. These may be all that are necessary to appeal to our listening brains. And so the variability in music in how the notes work together, flow rhythmically, and come into overall shape determines the type of music and the particular taste for it. As individuals we sense these differences keenly among the different types of music (even if it would be difficult to put them in words), but we also recognize that the sounds they make all belong in the realm of music.

Other art forms, such as literature, theater, and the visual arts, have their own complex array of genres and styles and adherents to each. But none of the others quite matches the broad appeal of music. Even literature, arguably the most popular of the other forms, does not engage the population as music does. Many read mysteries or romances, but not everyone picks up and reads books regularly, whereas virtually everyone today listens and responds to music voluntarily or involuntarily. Part of this difference may be that simply listening to music requires less effort than reading; also, music is ubiquitous in our culture and unavoidable day-to-day.

Beyond the degree of exposure and engagement, however, the emotional response of most people to music has a depth that all but the most ardent art lovers, readers of literature, and theater goers do not display. Consider the different responses of a room of concert-goers (in whatever genre) compared to a group that has gone through a museum. Now, there are many wonderful art collections, and contemporary museum practice has given us extraordinary special exhibits of great art that provide profound artistic experiences for many. But I wager that few have the emotional effect of a successful concert. Probably the art form closest to having this kind of effect without using music is live theater. A Greek or Shakespearean tragedy may drain us through its intended emotional catharsis, while a modern play such as by O'Neill, Beckett, or August Wilson may move us by shedding profound light on the human condition or social injustice. Most theater, however, does not sustain emotional impact the way music does throughout a performance.

The nearly instantaneous and sustained emotional effect of music is employed in many ways throughout our culture, both in other art forms and in commerce. Cinema makes ample use of music for emotional or dramatic effect. Some movies, such as "Jaws," "2001," and "Elvira Madigan," are known for their music and would not have been nearly as effective without it. But every movie since the silent era (which used live piano music to accompany it) has employed existing or freshly composed music to shape, reinforce, or anticipate the effects of the action. Musical theater takes this one step further by building song into the plot, much as does opera. In all these cases the range of emotions elicited by music is broad, including romance, mystery, foreboding, drama, heroics, joy, and even humor.

In our everyday world, permeated as it is with commercial messages, music plays a significant role in marketing products and inducing sales. Most advertisements on live media (television, radio) invoke music as background or the central theme. Skilled commercial composers know how to fashion the music to suit the product and the demographic to which it appeals. They must know what genre, form, and style to use even for a short piece lasting thirty seconds. While visuals are key, both in stationary advertisements and live media ones, the latter seem more like hard sells without musical accompaniment. Yet, the music undoubtedly makes the sales pitch more effective, even when we remember the jingle more than the product it promotes. For music conveys an important emotional message that becomes associated with the product. Because of the extraordinary range of musical emotion, music can reinforce the idea that a product improves one's attractiveness, provides romantic adventure, gives pleasure, or any number of other benefits that are often only tangentially (if at all) related to a product.

Music has enjoyed universal appeal in Western culture since at least Renaissance times, and by any measure it has flowered over the centuries in its many manifestations. Most other societies have their own music, but the sheer variety of ours makes one wonder if our civilization has a special ability to create and appreciate music. Suffice it to say that the West has a remarkably rich musical culture that attracts people from all over the world. Many top classical musicians in recent decades come from Asia, for example, while rock music appeals to young people just about everywhere.

Music in the West, we have seen, pervades the artistic, commercial, and entertainment aspects of our lives. It would be interesting to identify what, if anything, takes the place of music in less musical cultures. I suspect that any advanced civilization (such as those of China, Japan, or India) has other arts or cultural activities that provide an outlet for expression in accordance with that society. Music may be a part but not the predominant mode of such expression, which may be more concentrated in the visual arts or in language, to name a few alternatives.

To imagine the world without music at all, however, is to eliminate a significant aspect of modern civilization. One could walk the streets, be at home, or out on the town but never hear a note other than a car's horn or a bird's song. This may be a relief to the few who do not crave music in some form in their lives, and for all of us with regard to music we would rather avoid. For the rest, it would be like taking away our catnip, and we would become a sullen bunch, indeed. Of course, if we didn't know about music, we would certainly manage just as our prehistoric ancestors probably did. Our civilization has many other wonderful art forms and modes of expression that would engage us happily. We just wouldn't experience that sustained intensity and deep satisfaction that music can provide.

Perhaps what makes music universal and gives it such emotional power is its absolute quality, a purity detached from all else in our lives. Musical instruments, like art objects, are tangible, but the sounds that emanate from them are in a world of their own. That is why it is so difficult to describe music in words and why even the best verbal transcriptions and analyses fall woefully short. Great literature and art are also difficult to describe, but literary and art criticism do reasonably well in explaining their virtues. Even simple or frivolous music has a spirit and flow that cannot be matched by words that describe it. More similar is poetry whose rhythm and intonations mimic music, and indeed, in ancient times poets were essentially minstrels.

One indication of music's power and purity is its ability to stay with us afterward, sometimes for days or weeks. We may be moved by a play and haunted by certain scenes in it, but it will not likely replay in our minds the way music can. We can hear entire songs or parts of symphonies "silently" as we perform unrelated activities. At its extreme these "earworms" can be annoying. But music needs no scenes, no characters, no action to transpire in our auditory minds. As it does so, it continues to invoke the emotions and pleasures we associate with it. Music sustains itself within us as few other things do.

Leon Fleisher, the eminent American pianist, recently characterized music as "one of the most profoundly moving aspects of our civilization… it's forever challenging, it's forever ennobling."[2] He explained thus his lifelong involvement in music. For the rest of us who are not professional musicians or endowed as he is, music can still provide the values he eloquently expressed.

As a lifelong amateur and devoted student of music, I can well attest to the challenges music provides, particularly in playing it on instruments. Like anything difficult but rewarding, one can get frustrated and not want to continue practicing, only to have it come together and make the effort worthwhile. Attentive listening to music has similar rewards, particularly when the performers excel. One may not always feel ennobled, but one will usually feel uplifted and deeply stimulated by listening to music one loves.

All these qualities of music – emotional depth and sustenance, universal appeal, endless variety and originality – may be why I have an irresistible urge to share extraordinary passages of music I hear. I try to tamp the urge down, as I realize not everyone appreciates the particular kinds of music I do. It may also be difficult on first hearing to appreciate a piece, as it usually takes me several listenings to begin to grasp the magnificence of a complex work. Nonetheless, there I am, the proselytizer, trying to spread the sublime feelings I feel from great music.

---

[2] *Johns Hopkins Magazine*, Volume 70, no. 3, Fall 2018, page 19

The state of mind music can bring seems to me one of the truly wonderful aspects of life. I'm so glad we have ears that can hear complex sounds and an atmosphere that transmits them. What a luxury, too, that in the past century we can hear virtually any kind of music in our own homes (or on the road) through new technology. Our musical world is, indeed, a special and wondrous gift, as difficult as it is to describe it in words.

Driving (Me) Crazy

WHAT IS IT ABOUT driving a car that unleashes the worst instincts in people so as to endanger their lives and others'? What does this say about our society, and what will happen to this anger and aggression when self-driving cars take over?

I confess I have become something of a road wimp. I (mostly) adhere to the speed limit and eschew opportunities to joy-ride on highways and curves. I have seen too many accidents and heard of too many deaths and injuries by automobile not to make the connection and act accordingly. I remain mystified that my fellow humans do not do the same. Aggressive driving on the highways and near-universal speeding above already high limits make long-distance travel by car an exercise in dismal probabilities. I resent those who tailgate me on two-lane roads when I choose to maintain a safe speed. I've even had a few such maniacs nearly sideswap me and convey their displeasure digitally when they pass.

Aggressive driving today takes many forms, culminating in the extreme in road rage. AAA[3] and its foundation identify the following as aggressive: tailgating, speeding in traffic, cutting and weaving, running lights, and (the rage part) blocking, sideswiping, ramming, shouting/cursing/obscene gestures, forcing off the road, and confronting outside the car. Tailgating is the most common form of

---

[3] American Automobile Association; information in this paragraph taken from its "Exchange" website

aggression, estimated to be practiced by just over half of drivers in the U.S. Collectively, these actions have been found to cause half of fatal crashes.

It doesn't take much psychological insight to realize that people exhibiting aggressive driving use the power of the machine to express their pent-up frustrations and anger. Even mild-mannered people can turn into monsters behind the wheel. As a walker who has confronted many bad drivers as I cross streets, I can attest that using a car as a vehicle for one's anger cuts across gender, age, nationality, and race. Certain geographical areas are known for incubating vehicular aggression, but nowadays it can be found everywhere. No doubt greater urbanization with its attendant crowding, increased traffic, and interminable stoplights has exacerbated the problem. But anyone anywhere with serious frustrations in their lives may be susceptible to self-ignition when they get in their car. Being surrounded by a ton or more of metal makes one feel more secure in venting at others.

Besides today's crowded roads, another catalyst for aggressive driving is the otherwise bad driving that has also become commonplace. Examples include driving mindlessly in the passing lane, not signaling before turning, not staying within one's lane, not maintaining a steady speed, and being distracted while driving. Any one of these can set off an aggressive driver or annoy a decent one. But the proper response to bad driving is to distance oneself from it and even report it, not to engage in a match of misdeeds. Tailgating someone driving way under the speed limit or weaving around a wayward driver can only increase the chance of collision.

One of my pet peeves in bad drivers is the lack of turn signal. I may have acquired this chip honestly, as my father used to opine in disgust, "No signal, no nothing!" Fewer people nowadays seem to feel obligated to signal their intention to turn. Perhaps this represents an increased disregard for other drivers, a blocking out of the excessive number of cars, or a disconnection with one's own actions (a form of distraction). The lack of turn signal may sometimes cause accidents but more likely inconveniences other drivers who have to guess how neighboring cars will move. It is, admittedly, one of the least harmful of bad driving habits, but it is indicative of the inattention and lack of consideration prevalent on today's roads.

Aggressive driving goes beyond bad driving, as it is "performed deliberately and with ill intention or disregard for safety," in AAA's well-chosen words. The deliberate disregard for anyone's safety (including the driver's) distinguishes the aggressive driver's attitude from someone who is merely a poor driver. It also does not qualify as daredevil behavior, since that typically just affects the actor. Rather, it is like having an explosive on wheels amidst innocent drivers, who may well get caught in the conflagration it precipitates. It is, truly, not just reckless but also potentially criminal behavior.

That aggressive driving has become so common says something about our society. Our culture seems to accept a certain level of incivility on the road. Official policy is to warn and punish aggressive driving and counsel against engaging with it. But many drivers when confronted with aggressive driving feel the need to counter it in kind because they feel challenged. Their own anger and frustrations may be stoked, and the situation can escalate beyond control in the worst cases of road rage. We could, alternatively, envision a time not too distant, I hope, when this culture is reversed and, rather than taking the bait, people behave maturely when confronted. This response would put priority on human safety and decency rather than compensating for one's inadequacies with machine power.

Driving a car has another side that lends itself to reckless behavior. Despite all the rules of proper driving, despite the vagaries of traffic and road patterns, driving today's cars – with their power steering and braking, automatic transmission, quick acceleration, and smooth riding – seems quite easy and safe. In fact, driving appears easier than it really is, and people have a false sense of security until they experience an accident. Furthermore, most people don't appreciate the true danger in riding in a car, especially at high speeds. The crush of metal, glass, and plastic on human bodies, only partially protected by airbags, is never pretty. I remind my family that the energy in a collision (so-called kinetic energy) increases with the square of the speed, so that going from 65 to 75 mph actually increases the collision energy by another third.

I recall a lecture given by a visiting professor who studied automobile safety. She pointed out that a small error by a driver, akin to a slip of a knife in the kitchen, can have fatal consequences on the road. This could be an errant movement of the steering wheel or a missed glance in the sideview mirror. Particularly at high speeds, small moves (or lack of same) can have large consequences. That is why today's "distracted driving" – driving while checking or writing emails or texts (also, to some extent, talking on the cell phone) – can be devastating. Such stupid behavior as texting while driving assumes that driving requires minimal attention. Nothing could be further from the truth, especially on the highway.

One of the most exciting automotive developments in our lifetime is the ongoing development of self-driving cars, that is, vehicles that can automatically navigate roads and take passengers safely to any given destination. The development effort has been underway for several years, but as I write it is still in the experimental stage with only a few trials in actual road situations (a few of which have gone awry). There seems little doubt, however, that self-driving cars will become commonplace within the next decade.

Self-driving cars promise to drastically reduce accidents by virtually eliminating human error, which is the largest cause of vehicle accidents. Secondarily, traffic engineers believe that self-driving cars will allow much easier flow in congested areas by potentially reducing the space between cars and the idiosyncrasies of individual driving. What is not clear to me is whether self-driving cars will become the legal default or an option that can be overridden by a human driver. Current versions of partially automated cars necessarily include the override function in case the automation malfunctions. When automation is "perfected" (to the extent accidents are rare), will people still be able to override it and drive manually as they do today? If manual override is allowed and easily accessible, self-driving vehicles may do little to reduce aggressive driving.

The scenario of an aggressive driver in a sea of self-driving cars may not actually be likely, as their close spacing and "good driving" would seem to prevent such reckless movements. Also, the heightened control and bullying of aggressive drivers should be neutralized by a throng of non-human machines. What then becomes of the potential aggressor, relegated to a passive role in the vehicle? Will aggressive driving and road rage become obsolete and another channel found for suppressed frustrations and angers? Will domestic abuse soar and gun violence increase even more as a result?

Any answer to these questions would be speculative, although psychologists may have insight into the dynamic of anger transference. I suspect that some of the anger and frustration will find outlet elsewhere, as suggested. But I also believe that context can play a large role in whether anger and frustration are cultivated or more appropriately resolved. The current culture of aggressive and uncivil driving creates its own toxic cauldron, stirring up more anger and misbehavior. Eliminating this kind of environment may help tamp down angers and frustrations and allow them to be addressed in more constructive ways. Self-driving vehicles may not only reduce future traffic accidents but also make people calmer and more reasonable. If these are the result, I would gladly surrender my freedom to press the pedals.

Light and Water

WHAT IS IT ABOUT light and water that make them so magical? Do their special qualities give us insight into the hidden wonders of more mundane aspects of our world?

Loren Eiseley, scientist and writer, said that if there is magic on this planet, it is contained in water. Water is miraculous, if for no other reason than being the basis (along with carbon) for all life as we know it. As *in*organic as it seems in itself, water acts as a key constituent of living matter through photosynthesis and serves critical functions throughout biological and ecological systems. Even the non-living parts of the Earth's surface are mostly shaped by water acting on tectonically moving masses.

But Eiseley certainly had additional things in mind. Unlike most substances, water becomes less dense when it solidifies to form ice. This anomaly probably made life possible on Earth by protecting aquatic organisms from being frozen. As solid, liquid, or gas, water can also take many different forms, shapes, and colors. We talk of black ice and white ice, while the Eskimos have many different names for snow, depending on its texture. We experience dark and light clouds and fog or "mist" nearby. Lakes, seas, and oceans all differ in their color. Rainbows are among the more glorious manifestations of water, but any flowing water body draws our attention and, generally, admiration. Watching the surf at the ocean can entrance most of us for a long time. Waterfalls can draw people from across the globe.

Light is no less a requirement for almost all living things. Sunlight provides the energy for photosynthesis and keeps the Earth's surface and lower atmosphere at inhabitable levels. Most creatures living at or above the surface need light to function, even during the night (except for those with thermal vision or echolocation). For humans, life is defined by sunlight, with each day divided between daylight and night and gradations in between. We appreciate the dawn, dusk, and twilight, and note whether each day is sunny or cloudy. People like to bask in the sun's warmth and even change their skin color from it (often to their detriment). Sunshine connotes openness, freedom, and life itself, while dark of night is associated with bad deeds and evildoers or with unnatural beings and events that terrify.

The magic of light transcends its function as a daily need. We speak of glorious sunrises and sunsets, where sunlight produces striking colors and shapes as it is refracted through the atmosphere and clouds. The tandem of light and water also brings us the miracle of rainbows. In almost any non-degraded setting, the passing of the hours, days, and seasons provides unending variety to the same scene as light shines and reflects in different ways. Clouds contribute to these changes and add a further prism to the diurnal cycle of daylight. While few people other than artists notice the less spectacular effects of daylight, its constancy of change on Earth is truly fodder for our souls. The American painter Edward Hopper treated light as the essence of life that he probed through his work, and many others, such as Rembrandt, El Greco, and the French Impressionists, made light a central element of their art.

With both light and water, then, a key aspect of their magic lies in their dynamism. Water has so many different forms, and natural light has an infinite variety of appearances. But, equally, each unfolds in a dynamic way, with motion and continuity between different states. No matter how much one has experienced, moreover, a sensitive observer cannot fail to be struck by the continuing beauty of light and water in their various manifestations. The artist's job is to bring this to everyone's attention.

There are, of course, many other aspects of our world that have a dynamic character. A companion to light and water mentioned already is the atmosphere itself. But air cannot be seen, although its effects can be through wind. The solid earth is a dynamic in generally very slow motion, one that can be interpreted only by geologists and geographers. Plants and animals present an almost infinite variety of forms, and animals can fascinate us with their behavior and movements. But generally we treat the latter as part of our everyday world.

Yet, life itself is without doubt the most magical characteristic of our (living) planet. The forms and constituents of living matter have a complexity that even exceeds that of the inanimate world. That matter can compose itself to be alive and self-mobile; that it can grow and reproduce itself; and that it can feel, think, understand, and empathize, are all miraculous. We may not appreciate this in the throes of our quotidian existence, especially because we are part of the complex of life and sometimes in conflict with it. But it is surely a wonder.

It may be, though, that our appreciation of light and water is not much different from our indifferent attitude toward life around us. The aforementioned instances of light and water range from the commonplace (e.g., clouds) to the spectacular (e.g., rainbows), and most people show real interest only in the latter even though they may notice the former. In similar fashion, we generally don't pay much attention to the plants and animals around us unless we see something unusual, such as a flock of birds flying in formation. As artists open our eyes to the deeper effects of light, so do naturalists, biochemists, and poets enlighten us about the mysteries of living matter.

We distinguish the magical and the mundane in our world based more on the frequency of occurrence than anything inherent in it. The commonplace most of us treat as mundane; the exceptional, as worthy of our true interest. Yet, most everything in our world that is not degraded or corrupted has magic in it. As I wrote, now all is beautiful, so now would I write, all is magical. The wonders of a compound that takes so many forms, the magic of a radiative energy (both wave and particle) that travels at incredible speed, both combining in surpassing displays. The water and light that thus infuse our living planet add still more magic through the life they make possible in all its many forms and complexity.

Animal Emotions and Intelligence

WHAT IS IT ABOUT animals that makes it so difficult for humans to believe they have emotions similar to their own and a modicum of intelligence? And why are humans who love animals other than domesticated "companion" ones often considered misanthropic or averse to love of their own kind?

In the first case, it is stunning to what degree humans – even (or especially) very intelligent ones – are loath to concede to any animals the same kind of emotions and basic intelligence they have. They accuse one of "anthropomorphizing" animals, that is, imputing to animals the characteristics of humans. At best, they might concede that the "higher" animal species such as mammals and, particularly, primates – that is, those closest to humans – may partake of some emotions that resemble our own and have behaviors that appear to be learned or deliberate rather than merely instinctual. The sternest human chauvinists strictly rule out the possibility of self-awareness in other animals.

There are many sources for this attitude toward animals – historical, sociological, and even religious. Fundamentally, many humans need to believe in the inferiority of animals to justify the special status *Homo sapiens* has attained in the world order. In prehistoric times animals could be said to dominate over humans, a situation replicated later in the challenges faced by pioneers settling in the wilderness. The terror one might feel toward animals that could endanger one's person or property no doubt fueled the adversarial attitude humans developed toward other species. Seeing them as little more than a threat or source of food, it was imperative to gain control over wild animals and subjugate them (a process now considered, ironically, as the source of today's domesticated and companion animals). Treating wild animals as having feelings or thoughts only complicated matters.

As any animal lover or keeper of a companion animal knows well, animals such as the higher vertebrates do have emotions and their minds function beyond mere instinctual response. Animals are certainly more attuned to their instincts and may behave more instinctually overall than humans. They may not reason out a problem in order to overcome a challenge (not that many humans do). But there are numerous anecdotal and, increasingly, research examples where animals, including mammals and birds, solve complex problems, including by use of tools. This should not be a surprise. From an evolutionary perspective, deliberate consideration of challenges would be key to survival as organisms developed, so that merely instinctual fight-or-flight responses would not be sufficient to preserve the species. Many species besides humans have had the opportunity to develop more complex neurological responses, even though we attained an even higher level of conscious, rational thought thanks to an oversized brain.

The same holds true for animal emotions. This is a touchy area for human chauvinists, as they seem almost more willing to concede that animals can deliberate than that they can have feelings as we do. Perhaps it derives from the atavistic fear of identifying oneself as really just another kind of animal. As civilization developed, it became necessary to separate humans from the rest of the animal world to root out bad behaviors and instincts, often associated with (and projected on) animals. Also, to support the Western religious construct that humans derive from the divine, any suggestion of animalistic character would be anathema. In any case, our companion animals, including avians, canines, and felines, demonstrate amply to us that they can be joyful, sad, depressed, annoyed, angry, engaging, etc., that, in short, they can have expressive personalities. It is unlikely that these are merely learned behaviors or "parroting" to elicit desired human responses (which, in itself, is quite intelligent and does happen as well). Whether wild animals similarly experience such feelings may be largely conjectural, but I think the onus is on the doubter to show why not.

The artificial separation of humans from animals in terms of emotions and basic thought processes is reflected on the social level in the adverse reaction to people who profess a love for animals beyond the domesticated ones. Animal lovers so defined are often considered misanthropic, as if one cannot love other species as well as one's own. Protecting wild species and their habitats is instantly put in competition with taking care of human needs, which is society's priority. Ecological arguments about the need to preserve the web of life, including all other species, give ground to human primacy over creation and the implied intellectual and emotional inferiority of all other species. This is clear in the continuing assaults on the U.S. Endangered Species Act. Those humans who stand up for the rest of the biological world are, in essence, viewed as disloyal to their own kind.

There may be a kernel of truth about this attitude, but it is no doubt in reaction to the prevailing anthropocentrism of society. There is nothing wrong with humans putting a priority on their own needs, as all animals do to survive. It only becomes problematic when the needs of other species are completely subordinated to our own, because human impacts on other species and their habitats are far more extensive than comparable impacts by any other species. As the rest of the world's creatures have become the underdogs, those of us with an affinity for animals cannot help but sympathize with them and do everything to rectify the imbalance. Far from harming the human species, however, protecting the rest of nature and its intricate web of life is really the only way humans will stay healthy on this planet. So the reaction may admittedly be tinged with pique, but the result should be beneficial to all – human animals as well as all others.

Ever Hopeful

WHAT IS IT ABOUT life that makes me optimistic, despite all to the contrary?

I really am optimistic, although people who don't know me intimately might think otherwise. Optimists might express chagrin, despair, and negativity more often than others precisely because they expect more of life (and of other people, including themselves). Pessimists' lower expectations are generally fulfilled, giving them a kind of satisfaction, if not contentment. The vast majority of people in between – the complacent – take things as they come, with little thought or question.

But why be optimistic in the face of all the hardship and suffering that life brings, particularly at the hands of human beings? If we just faced the vicissitudes of the natural world, with its storms, floods, harsh weather, earthquakes, and disease (among other things), it would be challenge enough to maintain a positive outlook on life. Add to these interpersonal conflict and competition, social and economic inequality, racial animosity, bureaucracy, government oppression, and war (among other things) and the challenges to the optimist are overwhelming. Certainly, those who have suffered the most – the poor, the sick, the oppressed, and disadvantaged groups – have least cause to be hopeful.

Admittedly, I am not in the latter category. I have grown up and lived in material comfort in a wealthy country, given the best of education, and had a variety of career and personal opportunities. I may be frustrated that human society falls so short of the ideals it professes and that I am unable to fix this chronic failure. Yet, my worst despair is almost always counterbalanced by a fundamental belief that our time on Earth is a good, even wondrous thing.

How could this be? What wondrous states are revealed or promised here that could override the pervasive suffering, destruction, and often banality of life?

I do not believe in a heavenly state (or a hellish one) that earthly life is prelude to. I do not believe in a transcendental state on Earth that one may arrive at through studied practice (such as meditation), and in any case, it wouldn't be much help in solving society's ills. This does not, however, mean that I don't believe in an *ideal* state which we might strive to attain. And it appears that this ideal state is what propels my optimism about life.

Just what might this ideal state be, one might ask. And, if it is truly ideal and not likely to be realized, how can it actually support a sense of optimism?

Those who have grown up in certain Western cultures in the modern era have been exposed constantly to the moral "high road." The instruments of such acculturation include a wide variety of texts, principles, philosophies, value systems, social institutions, and religions that are based variously on moral principles. We are, in short, taught to be good, even though we come to learn that good behavior is not really that common nor is it necessarily rewarded by our peers or by society. That moment of realization of the disconnect between the ideals of Western society and its actual practice foments cynicism in many and a license in some to go to the dark side. Many people resignedly accept the dissonance as "real life," while others persist in striving for the ideal to be realized.

This gives some insight into the state in which I and some others find ourselves. Perhaps we were naïve when young and too obstinate and idealistic when grown-up to forsake what we so fully embraced earlier. Why, indeed, can't people act decently toward others and the rest of the world? Why must they hate and hurt, fight and kill, prove themselves more powerful and superior even when it has no real consequence? If some idealistic teachings may seem extreme (e.g., love your enemy, turn the other cheek always), surely the essence of decent behavior and the golden rule could be followed most of the time?

But this wishful optimism is about more than human behavior. The ideal state refers not just to a place where people are nice to each other, but to an exalted state of mind, a haven of the arts, and harmony with nature. It is an amalgam of the ideals of a liberal education in an uncorrupted and largely untroubled social context. It vaguely hints at a gentle communitarian arrangement (without actual group living) with the shared goals of intellectual, artistic, and spiritual fulfillment. Politics, small or large, plays no role in this state. Spiritual attainment is purely individual, and any association with established religion is kept private by the individual. Freedom of association, discussion, thought, and behavior (short of harming others) is assumed.

Even to this day, I carry on with this as an ideal, not necessarily expecting to realize it in my lifetime, but believing it to be what life could ultimately offer human beings. Of course, the ideal state neatly glosses over the myriad social, economic, and environmental problems that continue to plague mankind (or that mankind continues to plague the Earth with). This dissonance represents less a naïve disregard than a presumption that aligning with the ideal state will, *ipso facto*, lead to resolution of many of these problems. Here is where the "golden rule" – and various proliferations of it – factors into the ideal state to radically change our relationship to other human beings, other species, and the world around us (including animate and inanimate "resources"). But, in truth, such real-world problems have no place in the ideal state, whose issues are more of an existential, artistic, and spiritual nature.

As a child I would view bright, bulbous cumulus clouds as symbol of a beautiful state of being – not necessarily in the clouds, but transcendent of our secular existence. Since then, I have been above the clouds and seen within them (scientifically); yet, I am still drawn to this sign, and the condensed droplets and light they reflect still give me a kind of joy and assurance that life is worthwhile. My revered teacher and mentor admonished me long ago for my adolescent goal of living in an other-worldly, purely artistic existence. I have instead spent decades in the trenches of a *bona fide* career; yet, my dreamy goal seems to persist.

It is easy to believe that the worst characteristics of humans will continue to bring us down, that society will not ultimately achieve justice and equality, and even that artistic, philosophical, and spiritual pursuits are, in the final analysis, meaningless. Realists and pessimists avoid feckless hopes and disappointment this way. I instead choose to believe that the best in life is not yet at hand for most of us, nor impossible for us to achieve. It is largely within our grasp, should we agree to pursue it.

Chauvinism

WHAT IS IT ABOUT chauvinism, that people cling to it so, even though it is almost always an accident of birth?

By chauvinism, I mean the excessive, often irrational pride and partiality for the nationality, gender, race, or religion (etc.) an individual is part of or identifies with. In recent years the word has been used mostly to denote superior, discriminatory behavior by men toward women, but historically (and originally) it was used for patriotism gone amuck. Chauvinism is an undercurrent if not mainstream in most powerful or ambitious countries, and in recent years it has made a comeback after globalism held sway at the turn of the millennium. With it inevitably has come xenophobia, the complement to national chauvinism.

Yet, one only has to step back and ask, what if I came from a different country, even one considered an adversary? Growing up in the heat of the Cold War, I often pondered how I would feel if I had been born in Russia: would I have felt superior to and self-righteous toward Americans, as Americans felt toward Russians? The government would certainly have tried to make me feel that way through extensive propaganda, and with most citizens it probably succeeded, despite the deprivations they endured in the Soviet

Union. Russian nationalism is historical and deep-seated, and the same dynamic recurs today between the USA and a resurgent, post-Soviet Russia.

The accidental nature of one's affiliation in major groups might suggest the need for tolerance and understanding toward those with other identities. But such is not usually the case. The chance nature of identity gets subsumed by such phrases as, "Proud to be a(n) - _____," which emphasize the current and future state, not how it was derived. Regardless of whether being born an American was an accident, one is proud *to be* American and feels justifiably superior to others who *are not*, since this accident has conferred great privilege to those in the United States. And so forth regarding gender, religion, and other affiliations.

The tenuousness of chauvinism becomes blatantly clear with regard to gender. The chance aspect of one's gender could not be more apparent, despite the rare instances of gender change or the preference for a particular gender in countries like China. And yet, at both a societal and an individual level, the "battle of the sexes" goes on, based on chance drawings at conception. What makes this friction particularly fruitless is that both sexes obviously need each other for the species to continue, and friendship and love between the sexes is ubiquitous if not carefree. Certainly, the inequities that gender roles have produced over time in society must be rectified; where chauvinism sustains them, it must continue to be challenged. But fighting one gender's chauvinism with its counterpart is neither sensible nor productive.

Does this mean that men won't still complain about women, and women about men? Not likely. We all revert to a kind of tribalism, feeling most secure and comfortable in groups that are like ourselves. One could argue that this sense of tribal affiliation is not only necessary in humans but also beneficial if kept constructive and reasonable. Humans are generally a social species, and isolation can adversely affect mental health and behavior. Facing the vast, seemingly indifferent cosmos, or even just the impersonal life of a big city, most people need to feel part of something bigger than themselves but still within human scale. Affiliation groups can serve this purpose in a positive way that need not reflect negatively on others. Only when such groups assume a sense of superiority or antipathy toward other groups does this sense of belonging become chauvinistic or worse.

Still, one must ask why even a sub-chauvinistic level of friction occurs between human groups that are different in some respect. Why, for example, do men and women poke fun at or criticize each other's habits, behaviors, dress, talk, etc.? If roles were reversed, we would act the same as the opposite gender we joke about. But still, we can't help making sport of the difference, particularly as we age and have more experience with the opposite sex and its sometimes irritating differences.

In fact, sports gives a clue. Nothing could be more artificial in most cases than the group affiliation – otherwise known as fandom – engendered by professional or national sports. Teams based in a particular city are hardly rooted there, other than by playing roughly half the games at home. Players often live elsewhere outside of the season, and they are traded so frequently that the "home" team of one year may not resemble at all the one three or four years later. National teams, as in the World Cup or Olympics, normally consist of citizens of a particular country, but otherwise one has no connection to them, no more than one feels with all the other citizens in one's country. Yet, fans go crazy rooting for the home team and the national team; team chauvinism goes wild around the championship periods of a season or quadrennial event (in the case of the Cup or Olympics); and fan fervor sometimes gets out-of-hand and results in riots and worse.

Sports fan psychology plays out in mostly safe ways the atavistic tribalism of humans from ancient times, when a group with greater strength could dominate another. Fans in stadiums and bars act in ways they would never act at work or at home. When the opposing team is clearly superior to their own, fans nevertheless maintain their faith and loyalty until nearly the end, hoping that the "home" team will come through. The "visiting" team, coming from another city or country, is automatically suspect, its fans likely not very nice people, and any superiority it demonstrates questionable.

If sports are an avenue for the public to vent its chauvinism safely (as well as, of course, for true sports lovers to enjoy the play and strategy), the universality of sports and fandom suggests that there is a well of chauvinism within all of us that is always ready to spill out. When we are exposed to groups significantly different from us, we may instinctively compare them to ourselves to ensure we are equal or better. Chauvinism, even in its subliminal form, gives some comfort that we will probably survive after all.

Obstruction

WHAT IS IT ABOUT human institutions that makes them screw up or slow things down so much? And is there a fix for such?

"Bureaucratic" tells it all: as soon as an organization subdivides into units, interaction within and outside the organization becomes challenged. Procedures are developed but become a burdensome end in themselves. Lines of communication are established but are frequently violated. Roles and responsibilities are duplicated or left unfilled. Facts are massaged and sometimes concealed, but always a gloss coats messages to the outside world and to staff from management.

Worse is the effect of all this on those who work within. Having been educated to know their own thoughts, organizational workers are now expected to suppress their own views and follow those of their superiors. Having been encouraged (in America) to stand up for one's beliefs, workers are now bound to the doctrines of the company. And having been given lessons in truth-telling, bureaucrats and managers now find themselves talking in an acronym-ridden, truth-disguising techno-tongue unintelligible to the outside world.

The result of this dissonance is an employee selection process that can be contrary to the best interests of the institution and its workers. Compliance is generally rewarded over willingness to speak truth to power; taking the easy route over daring to experiment and possibly fail; adhering narrowly to one's own positional mandates over considering broader organizational, much less societal, goals. Consequently, those who rise in the bureaucracy tend to be "following leaders" – they don't make any major changes to their superiors' goals, just lead the rest along the same path. They also often exhibit self-protective tendencies to ward off dissenters and competitors inside and outside; back-stabbing is the unfortunate result in the most insecure and vicious.

With this operational and personal culture endemic to institutions, it is no wonder they struggle to get things right and take so long even when they don't. Every routine matter is split into myriad actions that get worked on by different units with their competing perspectives. Each stage provides opportunity for delay, disagreement, and error. When an extraordinary matter arises, it sends alarm bells throughout the bureaucracy because neither staff nor managers know how to deal with it and fear making mistakes or setting bad precedents. These matters are often shelved as a result, and the petitioners behind them wait for answers that don't come.

One may argue that human institutions need to operate this way, whether in governance, administration, or business. After all, if departments didn't exist with their specified functions, there would be even more chaos in anything bigger than a neighborhood grocery store. If managers and staff were truly empowered to go their own way and take initiative, policies and procedures that provide a modicum of order would be shortcut frequently and some institutions, such as in government or education, might not survive. The bureaucratic human could be a necessary part of the modern institution.

But surely no institution in a healthy society exists to slow down or obstruct necessary functions. That our modern institutions do so frequently is testament to their dysfunction. That's why we need the fix I am pleased to present here.

We must recognize, once and for all, that bureaucratic humans are indeed an essential part of modern life and train such persons to fulfill their functions properly. We have fancy schools for executives (business schools awarding MBAs) and training programs for mid-level managers. But nowhere do we spend the time to educate those who do the actual work in a bureaucracy.

We need, in short, a curriculum in bureaucracy. It should start at the pre-school and elementary levels and advance to the higher levels before long. It would cover the following topics in bureaucracy practice, based on the ills diagnosed above.

How to disagree with your superiors without their knowing

Staff should not always comply with directives from above, but instead should say what needs to be said and act accordingly. Managers, however, hate having staff disagree with them, no matter how much they pretend to encourage open discussion. In fact, most managers hold a grudge against any staff who disagree, sometimes for years.

Hence, bureaucracy school must instill in staff the art of disagreeing with managers without their realizing it. This is somewhat tricky but within the grasp of most bureaucracy students. The key is to ramble at length agreeably until the manager loses attention. Once a manager tunes out, their attention stays elsewhere for the duration, so staff can lay out their disagreements and follow them as if they received the manager's approval.

Appearing to tell the truth most of the time

All bureaucracies lie some of the time, as appears necessary for their survival. Lies are told both within and to the outside world; little ones euphemistically all the time, and big ones blatantly, as needed. All bureaucrats know they have to lie, but they feel bad about it because they were raised not to lie.

Hence, bureaucracy school must make students feel better about not telling the truth. Since lies must be told, school must train students to believe that most of their lies are truths. This is a tall order for most people, who are incapable of lying without sweating profusely and looking palpably guilty. They must realize that evasions are legitimate expressions of bureaucratic positions and, as such, truthful in their own right. They must be trained not to feel uncomfortable if they don't tell the whole truth or deliberately confuse or mislead their audience. These are, after all, prevarications, not lies. So in the grand scheme the bureaucrat is telling the truth most of the time, as outright lies are few.

Suppressing your own beliefs while accepting organizational doctrine

Once students learn the previous lessons about truth-telling, it is an easy sequel to train them to believe that the organization's doctrines are really their own. First, bureaucracy students must undergo a thorough purging of all their previous beliefs in all areas, organizational and personal, particularly regarding the subject areas covered by the institution. Once students are sanitized, they will be a tabula rasa for the organization's doctrines. This process is repeated numerous times in bureaucracy school so that students can perform it automatically upon being hired.

Making recommendations for innovation without ever failing

We pointed out above that bureaucracies discourage experimentation because of the possibility of failure, which dooms a bureaucrat's career. Workers instead choose the easy route, which may not be the most effective in solving a problem or warding off the competition. The solution is a course that teaches students how to devise known solutions in the guise of being innovative, satisfying the organization's professed support for innovation. An important part of this course also shows students how to rig roles and responsibilities so that failure always falls on another unit in the organization.

How to bury extraordinary business and make the petitioner forget about it

Nothing intimidates bureaucracies more than the extraordinary, since they are designed to deal with the routine. Hence, bureaucracy school must teach how to make unusual requests from the outside disappear. While this process is already innate in most bureaucracies, it must be done in such a way that the outside petitioner no longer thinks about pursuing the matter.

This can be accomplished in two ways. Because extraordinary matters must be considered outside the normal bureaucratic channels, the student is taught how to load on the review chain until it is longer than the routing slip (whether hard copy or virtual). At the end, the petition will disappear in the bureaucratic ether, but only after many months or years have gone by. The other way is to promise the petitioner a particular solution but never follow up on it; when the petitioner calls back periodically, the promise is repeated with greater assurances until ultimately the caller forgets to call back. I know this approach works, as it has happened to me.

Avoiding bureaucratic errors and speeding up bureaucratic processes by working less

What annoys people most about bureaucracies is not just that they take so long to do anything, but that they usually get the result wrong. The solution is clear, but as before, it runs against the grain. Reason tells us that delays result from bureaucrats working on a matter, and errors in handling the matter also result from bureaucrats working on it. Therefore, the logical solution is to have bureaucrats work less. The challenge is that they do not want to look like lazy bureaucrats and would refuse to work even less than they normally do.

The curriculum will address this conundrum by teaching students how to do half the normal work while working busily the entire time. This is something of an art form that is best reserved for the higher levels. Students will be taught the technique of writing elaborate reports with complicated matrices detailing the status of each project, thus substituting reports for actual work. Managers will be impressed and take the reports as proof of real work. With half the actual work being performed in the bureaucracy, fewer delays and errors will result.

Back-stabbing made easy and undetectable

The reader will forgive me if the mention of back-stabbing above suggests that only managers practice it and only those who are bad human beings. In fact, everyone indulges in back-stabbing, especially in an organization. It's just that some people are better at doing it than others, who leave their prints all over the victims' backs.

Hence, bureaucracy school must teach students how to be effective at back-stabbing, especially in concealing themselves as perpetrator. Courses will provide the necessary theoretical foundation to show that bureaucratic survival and advancement require that your peers are denigrated, leaving fewer candidates for the few top positions. Practical tools will be given along with simulated exercises to demonstrate how best to undo your colleagues without their knowing it. Equally important and previously unmentioned is instruction on how to prevent yourself from being taken down by others; this will require constant spying on your colleagues and eavesdropping on managers, and thus is probably best reserved for the graduate level.

In conclusion, obstruction may be a chronic feature of human institutions. But it need not get in the way of necessary societal functions or warp the essential human character of those who work in them. The bureaucracy school proposed here resolves most of the problematic issues and, as a bonus, produces workers who are better prepared than most to succeed in this world.

Weather

WHAT IS IT ABOUT the weather that it can be both so influential and so ignored and belittled? Would we want to control the weather we get, and what would be the result if we could?

Unless there is a weather "event," we generally ignore the weather except to introduce our conversations or fill in pauses. Talking about the weather is often considered a substitute for more substantive discussion. Worse, it has the stigma of mental sterility, as devastatingly stated by Oscar Wilde: "Conversation about the weather is the last refuge of the unimaginative." For weather, ubiquitous in our lives, is an easily fetched topic when nothing else comes to mind or a social situation hangs awkwardly. It is a favorite topic of small talk, the social chatter exchanged between people who don't know each other well enough to go deeper.

This is, however, an incomplete characterization of weather and of those who talk about it. I happily counter with another quote by an equally eminent writer, Marcel Proust: "A change in the weather is sufficient to recreate the world and ourselves." Certainly, weather can be a diversion from matters that may more directly pertain to us. But it is, after all, the way our world – the environment in which we live – presents itself to us each moment of each day. It is also a link to the beauty of the world and its dynamism and power. Weather does have the power to remake our surroundings, even in its tranquil states, as a rainy day can be completely different from a sunny one. Gray, drab, washed colors can have their own kind of beauty, one that is completely different from the brilliance of a yellow-splashed day.

The various conditions and changes of weather can also profoundly affect our mood and state of mind. Who has not brightened up on a sunny day following days of rain or fog? Who does not feel relieved by calm, cooling rain after days of dry heat? The degree to which one is affected by daily changes in weather undoubtedly depends on the individual, and most people may not be conscious of any effect in the normal course of weather changes. This does not mean that weather does not subliminally affect us all. There may even be a weather equivalent to those who are affected by the change in seasons (seasonal affect disorder), in that their mood is inordinately affected by the daily weather. In any case, almost all of us have had the experience of waking up to a bright, beautiful day and feeling reinvigorated or sensing that a venture begun on such a day is auspicious.

The normal swings of weather can affect our daily routines and activities. Outings such as hikes, sports, exercise, or picnics depend on a modicum of "decent" weather. Rain dates are scheduled in case "bad" weather occurs when outdoor group events are planned. Even going places in a car, whether for local shopping or sightseeing trips, can be altered by weather that is not conducive. When it comes to activities we may want to avoid, weather is often a convenient excuse for not participating. Routine weather can even have serious consequences, such as when rain suppresses voter turnout for elections.

So much more is the effect of weather events that are extraordinary or extreme. These include snow and ice storms, torrential rain, hurricanes, tornadoes, deep freezes, and heat waves. Now everyone pays attention, with a newfound respect and fear for what was previously dismissed. Grocery stores get raided in many of these cases, with people favoring milk, bread, and toilet paper for their survival. Broadcast media and the Internet are flooded with news about the weather event, as forecasts are continually updated with graphic pictures of the unfolding event. In the worst cases, weather can have catastrophic consequences in destroying property, lives, and natural features. It is not true, as someone once said, that all weather is good.

Nevertheless, the prevailing attitude toward weather is indifference. Many of us don't seem to notice it consciously unless it is extraordinary or directly affects our activities. I am sometimes struck by the degree of this unawareness even when something remarkable is happening in the sky. One morning after a rainstorm I came onto the train platform going to work to find a gorgeous rainbow in the west. But only one other person out of dozens noticed and marveled at the feature. (She and I smiled at each other as if we had a secret too good not to share.) So, too, magnificent clouds and skyscapes or brilliant light can be ignored or dismissed. No doubt people have immediate, personal concerns that make these extraneous weather features insignificant.

Yet, our sages and seers have thought otherwise about weather and related atmospheric events. Weather can figure significantly in literature, where authors as great as Shakespeare mirror the plot or foreshadow events to come with storms, lightning, blackening skies, and such. Weather is linked to the human condition in these references, whether the author uses it for symbolic purposes only or believes in a real relationship between them. Certainly, on the superstition side, events like eclipses and earthquakes were historically thought to portend disaster, while more common weather events were also treated as omens in many cases, and still are to this day. Thus, we say that misfortune "rains down" on someone, while good fortune "shines" on one, signaling our supposition (or superstition) that sunny days are more auspicious than rainy ones.

We owe our weather, with its constant changes and surprises, to several geophysical factors. Foremost is the presence of a gaseous atmosphere that transmits heat and moisture. This alone would not be sufficient to produce the continual variety we experience, which is caused by the differential heating the atmosphere receives from the Sun. The Earth's rotation and revolution guarantee that every part of the Earth's surface has its day in the Sun. The mostly spherical shape of the Earth causes differential heating at all times, depending on the latitude and season. And the prevalence of water on the Earth's surface (covering about 70% of it) – a compound that can be liquid, vapor, or solid within the range of Earth's temperatures – ensures further discrepancies in heating and evaporation between land and sea. These differences move air and water vapor around the globe and between layers of the atmosphere to produce wind, precipitation, and air masses with different characteristics, causing day-to-day weather.

But what if our weather were not to change much – what effect would that have on us? It so happens there are regions of the Earth where weather fluctuations are minimal, at least compared to others, and they might give a clue. Along the southern California coast, the difference in the average high temperature between summer and winter is a mere eleven degrees; while rainfall falls almost exclusively in the winter, it only amounts to ten inches annually. Even more uniform is the weather in many tropical areas. Temperatures there can fluctuate as little as a few degrees over days and even seasons. While the tropics often experience a rainy and a dry season, the rainy season can be prevalent and persist most of the year.

I don't know if this question has been studied at all with reference to these locations of relatively uniform weather. So I'll just venture a few comments based on my limited experience. Where the weather is uniformly "good," such as in San Diego, many people respond positively, particularly if they enjoy outdoor activities. After all, they can go outside almost all the time and play in the water, sand, or land. Occasionally one might hear a negative or nostalgic comment about missing the seasons (typically from a transplanted Easterner) or being bored by the monotony of the beautiful weather. In tropical zones where conditions, though uniform, can be less comfortable – such as high humidity and rainfall – the same kind of affection may not be granted to the local weather. Those from the tropics who migrate north may not appreciate the cold, snow, and ice, but otherwise they do not seem to wax nostalgic about the heat and humidity at home.

This question brings up a broader one: what would it be like if we could control the weather? There are many aspects to explore here, including whether we would be technically capable of controlling the weather in the future; if so, whether we should control the weather, and to what degree; who would decide what weather any location would have; what controls would be put on extreme weather events; and how we would respond to predictable, and presumably more benign, weather. These are all meaty topics, so just a few thoughts on each here.

So far humans have shown virtually no capability to control or intentionally affect the weather. Ironically, we are much better at affecting global climate, although we have done so inadvertently and, largely, harmfully. At best, under certain favorable circumstances we can induce clouds to precipitate their moisture by seeding them. As to harnessing the large air masses that swirl constantly around the globe and produce our weather, the energy required would be massive, far beyond what we currently have available. One could envision in the distant future, when solar energy is our primary source of energy, that the atmosphere could be "wired up" like the Earth's surface and controlled thereby. In the meantime, controlling, mitigating, or eliminating destructive weather phenomena like hurricanes and tornadoes would be sufficiently challenging but not impossible if the appropriate device could be applied. Perhaps a controlled explosion in the "nerve center" of such cyclones might do the trick.

Whether weather should be under human control, in what way, and by whom are delicate ethical and social matters. Our first impulse may be to respond resoundingly in the affirmative to the first, until we realize the implications and complications involved. Even more deeply, we may question the wisdom of taking one more step in making nature subject to humankind, as we have profoundly done on the Earth's surface and to many of its creatures. A completely tamed atmosphere would be yet another closure of a spiritual avenue that doesn't involve other humans. It would be the sky equivalent of losing woods to walk in.

Imagine, too, the difficulties involved in determining what weather each location would get. Would there be referendums in each place with a menu of weather options within a particular climatic zone from which to choose? Would we rely on "experts" such as meteorological psychologists (a new discipline) to help determine the optimal mix? How would one location's weather decisions potentially impact another's, and how would resulting conflicts – such as over rainfall scarcity – be resolved? Who, ultimately, would make weather decisions and at what level? I fear the complexities involved would be far beyond our society's ability to make decisions.

On one control we may all agree: tempering the destructive force of extreme weather events. As much as we may not want to "humanize" the weather, no one wants to be victim to hurricanes, tornadoes, and ice storms. If we found a way to weaken these events, would we not have an obligation to do so? Again, the difficulty would be in determining at what level controls would be placed. Would all hurricanes be downgraded to more benign tropical storms, or even the latter prevented? Ice storms no greater than one-quarter inch accumulation on branches? No tornadoes at all, since almost all are severely destructive? How, indeed, would we avoid making the weather in our own image under these scenarios?

In the ultimate scenario of complete weather control, which would presumably be more benign and uniform, our current indifference to the weather would likely become complete. Weather would be a complete background to our lives, never intrusive, always predictable. While "inclement" events might still have to be scheduled to replenish surface water and groundwater from rainfall, they could be confidently scheduled around. I suppose those who don't ordinarily pay much conscious attention to the weather or value the changing atmospheric display wouldn't feel deprived; probably, they would appreciate the greater convenience of planned weather. For those of us who delight in the vagaries of the sky and what it brings, such control could be devastating, causing permanent weather affect disorder. For although we wouldn't want anyone hurt from extreme weather events, we would sorely miss the added dimension of variety and unpredictability the weather provides. We might also have more trouble starting a conversation.

Every Day

WHAT IS IT ABOUT our everyday tasks that makes them so necessary and yet so variable among individuals? And how do we learn, acquire, and remember to do them?

The subject here concerns all those quotidian personal and household chores that face us each morning, including taking care of hygiene and arranging things in the home. For those on a strict commuting schedule, these tasks are usually conducted automatically before leaving. The routine doesn't vary much and is designed to get everything done in a short time. Others with more flexibility go through similar, if elongated, routines.

One may wonder how much of these bustling daily activities are really necessary. Certainly, some of them are critical, and some can be missed or delayed. People turn back from their commute when they forget to put on their eyeglasses or turn off the stove. But they'll likely live with the consequences of not brushing their teeth in the morning or leaving the lights on in the kitchen. Everyone who goes out the door has to get dressed, at the very least, but beyond that the range of tasks conducted at home varies greatly. Some people put on makeup in the car or eat their breakfast on the train.

While it is never good to be sick, it does afford a change in perspective from our daily routine. We forgo many of these activities when sick in bed, and mysteriously they no longer seem so necessary. Those related to work or the daily commute obviously fall away, but so do many others we habitually and strictly perform, including personal hygiene. Of course, the latter cannot be postponed too long without unpleasant consequences.

One may wonder, too, how much of the daily routine is by design. More organized individuals have a mental list of what they need to do each day, but even this may be amorphous and followed somewhat randomly. If the routine follows a set sequence over time, it can become automatic and honed for efficiency. Less organized people approach their tasks in a more haphazard way that ensures some may be forgotten or squeezed out by time. But they seem not to care as much, blessed as they are with insouciance.

Differences in what each individual does in the daily routine and in the amount of time spent on these tasks correspond to a surprising degree to the organizational proclivities of the person. The more organized tend also to be fastidious about their daily routines, covering more tasks and making sure each is done thoroughly. The less organized, already prone to forgetting about or having no time for some tasks, tend to do fewer of them and in a more casual, even sloppy, way. The range of these differences can be startling, even among siblings who have a common upbringing. One may spend fifteen minutes preening in front of a mirror, the other not a minute; one may meticulously arrange many toiletries (covering multiple functions) on the dresser, the other spread a few necessities randomly around the room (and floor).

This raises the question of how we learn or acquire our daily routines. Parental direction is the starting point, but this example demonstrates how variably the information is incorporated in children. Their personality and constitution certainly affect what filters through. Peers and roommates are another important source, coming into influence just when children begin to be responsible for these tasks on their own. In fact, with the natural aversion to follow parents' advice, young people are more likely to look to outside models for their behavior, including grooming, hygiene, and housekeeping. Commercials in the media factor in significantly as well, as many feature just these daily tasks and the products employed in them, demonstrated by other young people.

As young people mature, they form their own judgments about self-care and managing their households, and their routines take on a more individualistic character. This has real consequences, as it may limit the compatibility of an individual for living with someone else, whose routine may be very different and clash with the other. This is a not infrequent occurrence with roommates and even with married couples, especially those who get together later in life. For people in middle age can be set in their ways, which include – very importantly – the ways they do their daily routines. Probably the most common conflict occurs over different levels of household neatness, but problems also arise over different waking and sleeping hours and bathroom habits. Friction over small tasks can, in fact, take on a much larger significance if it symbolizes a deeper conflict between individuals living together.

It is odd how strongly individuals can adhere to the particular ways they do their routines. They see them as necessary to their welfare, and in aspects like personal hygiene some tasks are. They insist on getting them done each day and can get peevish if their routine is delayed or impeded. Particularly in older people, the daily routine becomes an important aspect of their lives, as other things like career drop off and as the daily tasks to which they are accustomed become more difficult to do. For many, their everyday routine helps define who they are, and it becomes as personal as their fingerprints.

As I wake up in the morning, I sometimes wonder how we remember to do the daily tasks each day and in what order. Some require no conscious thought because our bodies demand them. Others are "elective" but become habitual through so many repetitions. Still, there is discretion as to when these are done. If we are not completely in automatic mode, we can choose when to make the bed (if we do) or brush our teeth. What occurs in our brains to present these tasks to our consciousness each day? It is some kind of cognitive function, and it can weaken or disappear with old age and dementia.

I well remember when my maternal grandmother, who was then living with us, came out of the bathroom one morning. She had soap all over her face she had forgotten to wash off. My parents looked ruefully at each other, and before long they decided she needed the care of a nursing home. Her daily routine was in the hands of others thereafter.

Raising Children

WHAT IS IT ABOUT raising children, that it can bring such a mix of joy, sorrow, satisfaction, worry, wonder, and perplexity? Is the human experience of child-rearing normal or an anomaly in the Animal Kingdom?

Although in most cases we make a deliberate decision to have children and raise them, the force behind this intent is by no means fully conscious. At work is the procreative urge, the desire to reproduce. Procreation is, of course, a complement to libido, but the latter does not necessarily encompass the former. Those who have been driven by both know that the procreative, while perhaps less intense, can be more profoundly powerful.

Because procreation is built into our genes, everything it involves is laden with special force. This drive continues after children are born, perhaps even more strongly, as parents switch gears into nurturing mode. Like other animals, we are driven to care for our young until they are deemed independent. In the human species this involves an obligation that continues for many years after birth. Over such a long time we develop strong bonds with our children that usually persist through the parents' lifetime.

Emotions of all kinds can be involved in raising children and can manifest themselves in surprising ways. On the good side, this can elevate the experience and make it uniquely rewarding. Helping our children grow and develop fully can bring joy and pride that eclipses what one might feel about one's own life. Watching a child develop skills and possibly become very proficient at something makes one feel a sense of accomplishment, like giving something additional to the world. Having children invariably brings one closer to one's community, whether through schools, neighbors, or places of worship. Some of these connections provide lasting friendships for parents, too. And one of the unsung joys of parenting is that one can relive aspects of one's own childhood. In concrete terms, this happens when one participates directly in a child's games or activities. More deeply, one can better understand one's own childhood by being involved in the unfolding experiences of one's children.

On the negative side, raising children can cause untold stress and a range of unpleasant emotions like sorrow and anxiety. No one goes through parenting without experiencing difficulties, whether from illness, behavior, accidents, or problems at school. The worst can be devastating, such as loss of a child or a life-threatening illness. More common parental challenges include difficult behavior at various developmental stages or inability to deal with social norms, including expectations at school. As the child gets older and more independent the worries can grow, particularly in the teenage period when so many temptations and pitfalls present themselves to the impressionable young person. Parental anxiety never disappears, even with an adult child, and grandchildren can add new subjects to worry about.

These stresses, along with the routine commitments required of parenting, can have significant effects on other relationships, starting with the spouse or co-parent. Arguments are common over parental duties and whether one parent has an unfair share. Problems that arise with children can cause disagreements between parents as to cause and solution. Sometimes these situations reveal fundamental rifts between parents that were not previously apparent, or else they unearth residual issues from their own childhoods that compel responses that are incompatible with each other.

Parenting can also have significant effects on relationships outside the immediate family, particularly with friends. As my college friends formed families before I did, I experienced a serious reduction in my connection to them. Their time got swallowed up by parenting duties, and my time with them became negligible in many cases. Even correspondence by letter (email was non-existent at the time) dropped off precipitously. I tried not to repeat this when I became a parent, but probably did the same to my friends. Conversely, having children can bring one closer to extended family, as one has a renewed focus on family and a desire to foster relationships between one's children and their grandparents, cousins, uncles, and aunts.

While all these events and changes are happening, a parent's outlook on life and the future often undergoes a profound transformation. The young adult – as most parents still are – who focused previously on job, career, mate, and entertainment now is equally concerned with the world into which the children are being raised. Mostly in broad rather than political terms, parents begin to worry about the state of the world, their country, or their community. Thinking about the future changes from an abstract, distant irrelevancy into concrete documents securing financial security, life insurance, mortgage, and college savings accounts. Parents begin to realize their own mortality more clearly; concomitantly, they see themselves as part of a long chain of human generations. In this sense, raising children constitutes an important human legacy all parents give to the world, and it can provide great satisfaction that the childless must find elsewhere.[4]

The change in perspective occurs in other ways, too. Young adults generally have an independent if not rebellious attitude toward their parents' generation and established society. While this may continue in a political way and initially in their parenting as they attempt to do things their own way, sooner or later most young parents find themselves acting as their parents did. Often this comes as a shock as a young parent will say something to their child or act in a way that their mother or father did. And it can be highly imitative, to the word and tone, not just reminiscent. This role reversal comes about naturally because they are, after all, now parents as well. But it also signals a change in outlook that inevitably comes from the new role and responsibilities. Depending on what is being acted out, it may engender a greater appreciation for the parent's parents.

---

[4] I am indebted to my friend JP Kusz for this idea in a conversation some years ago.

With all these complexities involved in raising children, it is no wonder there are many theories about how to do it properly. These range from traditional approaches handed down orally from generation to generation to formal child-rearing and child development philosophies coming out of modern psychology and medical science. Among the most famous practitioners in the second category are Drs. Spock and Brazelton. Traditional methods come courtesy of one's own parents, friends, nosy strangers, and, inevitably, one's mother-in-law. Many expectant parents, particularly among the more educated, read up assiduously on the most popular parenting theories and practices. Nowadays there are myriad volumes from which to choose, often in conflict with each other. A confused and frustrated parent may very well conclude that using common sense and following their gut are the best guides to raising their own child.

It is also no surprise that *Homo sapiens* would make child-rearing such a complex enterprise with seemingly no right answers or universal practice. Here is where instinct truly vies with "knowledge" and reason. Regardless of how intelligent other animal species are, their child-rearing appears to follow rather strict pathways for each species, and so they are probably following instinct most of the time. Humans gave that up long ago as the sole determinant of parenting. Even though some other species also have strong social groups that participate in child-rearing, they do not seem to anguish about it the way we do.

Rearing a human child takes much longer than comparable development of other animal species because our brains take so long to develop. Unlike precocial animals, which can function and care for themselves virtually right after birth, human babies are essentially helpless for years. Even the Biblical coming of age at twelve or thirteen requires many years of parenting; in modern times, this has extended to at least sixteen if not later. The young of some other species may stay with the parents for a few years and even help in rearing succeeding broods, but none sticks around to the extent humans do, even as a proportion of their lifespan (orangutans come close, but they are very like us, too). Consequently, human parenting is a very long commitment. While this presents an additional burden on parents, it also fosters lifelong relationships between them and their offspring that do not seem prevalent in other animals.

As the parent of two now-grown children, what was most surprising to me was the range of experiences and emotions this long child-rearing evoked. I suppose there are some families where childhood is calm and crises are very few, but I don't know of any personally. Growing up in such a roller coaster can be emotionally challenging as well, but as a child one knows little else. As a parent, one might expect greater control over the situation and a smoother trajectory, but these are rarely attained. Instead, one embarks on an endlessly repeated but always unique experiment to recreate the human world, preferably for the better. One can only hope to reap for one's family as much joy, growth, and fulfillment as the vicissitudes of life allow.

Nature's Cruelty

WHAT IS IT ABOUT nature, that it can be so cruel that the pain and existence of individual animals are virtually irrelevant?

The very topic and opening sentence require immediate clarification. We may speak of nature's cruelty as if there is intention in nature and deliberate indifference or hostility toward its creatures, but this is not likely the case. We personify nature to more easily describe it; in reality, nature is the interaction of myriad physical and biological entities and forces. If we actually ascribe a motive to natural events, we are projecting on nature anthropomorphic qualities or theistic beliefs about its workings. Otherwise, we refer figuratively to nature's effects. With this understanding, we can proceed with the collective, personified use of the term nature.

That nature can be harsh on the individual animal cannot be gainsaid. Merely to survive in the wild means dealing with potential scarcity of food and shelter, competition, diseases and injury, adverse weather, and predators. Animals in the wild seem to be on constant alert for any threats. Even predators may be another's prey and have no assurance of finding their own. It is a wonder to see animals cope with extreme cold or heat; a portion undoubtedly does not survive each winter or heat wave, although wildlife deaths are often hidden from us. Animals that are injured, diseased, or malnourished have a much lower chance of survival, and one can only imagine the suffering they endure while they await their end. For those struck by a predator, it is not always true that their demise is instantaneous, as one can attest from experience and wildlife films.[5]

Ecologists would say that nature's interest is in preserving the species, not the individual. The propagation of a species usually involves multiple offspring in order to ensure a sufficient number survives to continue the species. Many fish, amphibians, arthropods, and insects produce large numbers of fertile eggs, of which only a small portion survives into adulthood. Some bird species even countenance infanticide to enable the strongest of the clutch to grow up and reproduce. Nature, it seems, plays the numbers game with species: if there are enough individuals in play, enough will survive to maintain the species. Too bad for the others.

Yet, nature can be equally callous with respect to the survival of a species. There is no safeguard when the number of individuals in a species gets below a critical level, and natural changes in the environment happen without regard to their effect on plants or animals. Mass extinctions have occurred a number of times over Earth's history due to cataclysmic events like widespread volcanism, climate change, or major meteor impacts. These events may result in upwards of ninety percent loss of species extant on Earth. Under more typical evolutionary conditions species drop out over time as well. Ironically, species extinction usually occurs over an extended period and does not necessarily cause the intense pain and suffering individuals can otherwise confront in their lives.

What drives nature is not to preserve anyone or anything but to continue to evolve. Change is said to be the constant of life, and with

---

[5] For more on predation and its implications, see the essay, "Death and Predation."

the variable forces in nature, that inevitably happens over time. Natural processes, fueled by energy from outside and within the Earth, occur continuously. The result is evolution both of the physical Earth and of all its living forms. But nothing drives such evolution toward a particular result, remarkable as its products have been over hundreds of millions of years. We do know that evolutionary adaptations that increase survival and reproductive success are favored. Some biological organisms and systems have become more organized and complex over time, while others have remained simple to best survive. All of them could be wiped out instantly by collision with an extraterrestrial body. So nature as a whole hardly safeguards any specific part of itself.

This all seems like a harsh, haphazard way to run the world, with individual organisms bearing the brunt of it. But the world *is* haphazard in terms of events and effects. There are causes for each, but no overall plan on the direction they should go. Things happen as a result of physical forces, and the trajectory of each action has its place in time, whether momentary or geologic. Weather events occur day-to-day; tectonic forces like earthquakes and volcanism on the order of decades or centuries; and cosmic events like the Big Bang and expanding universe over billions of years.

To this cosmic chaos was added several billion years ago the molecules and then the cellular and organismic structures to form living beings. We do not know whether life emanated from Earth or beyond, nor whether life on Earth is unique in the universe. But, aside from creating the conditions to form carbon-based life, nothing in the universe appears "designed" to encourage or nurture life. And just because conditions were conducive to life on Earth does not mean life did not have difficulty establishing itself here. Even so, conditions in many places on Earth remain hostile to life, and at times conditions anywhere on Earth can be inhospitable. Yet life has certainly eked out an existence on Earth, and it has done a pretty good job at it, considering how widespread living organisms are on the Earth's surface and in the oceans. Despite sometimes harsh conditions, life has a tenacity that keeps it growing and coming back. Like an army, life maintains itself overall, but often at the expense of individual beings.

Could one design a system *de novo* whose goal is to promote life, species and individuals alike? Would this overcome nature's "cruelty" and still be viable? The answer is probably yes, but the result would contain far fewer species, life forms, and adaptations. Starting with environmental conditions that are optimal for a wide range of species, those that thrive at the extremes could not exist. Also, some species thrive on the very conditions or events that limit others; for example, natural forest fires may unleash certain plant species while suppressing others. Eliminating predation, disease, and environmental changes would slow evolution and adaptations, and the tree of life would have far fewer branches as a result. This might be a utopia for a limited number of species and their individuals, but one cannot be sure that the ecosystems thus formed would provide what Earth currently does for its inhabitants.

For, cruel as nature can be to individuals, life on Earth has evolved in a way that supports a multitude of species and their ongoing representatives. Life in nature may often be "nasty, brutish, and short," as Thomas Hobbes stated, but it isn't always so. For humans and, there is reason to believe, for many animals, life can bring substantial pleasures and beauties as well. The human arts, stretching back millennia, are testament to the benefits we reap from life beyond mere survival and reproduction. There is also good evidence that many vertebrates participate in play activities. Whether they also appreciate the beauty of nature, as we imagine songbirds do when they sing on a lovely spring morning (for procreation), may be beside the point. Animals are not necessarily under duress all the time. Most also know how to rest or just hang out. Life on Earth may not always be "good" or gentle, but it need not be considered chronically cruel.

Human Waste

WHAT IS IT ABOUT human beings across history and societies that causes them to create so much waste in all their endeavors? Is there a need to produce waste or to pursue practices that inevitably create it? And is there any hope for a solution?

Before addressing these questions, let's examine the opening postulate that human beings create excessive waste. Do we, in fact, produce more waste than other animal species? Certain insects (locusts, grasshoppers, gypsy moths) can lay waste to entire fields and forests, and beavers can nearly clear-cut portions of riverine forests, which they then flood. Nature itself, through large-scale phenomena like floods, fires, earthquakes, and storms, can devastate large areas that must be restored. When it is said that humans have become a geological force, the implication is that natural dynamics are already producing much of the change we do, including "destructive" events.

But there are significant differences between all these natural or animal effects and those of humans. For one thing, animal impacts are rarely on the scale of human ones. A species may extirpate another species, but humans tend to do so more quickly and in greater abundance. The difference holds even in prehistoric and classical times, where humans are known to have had significant impacts on the landscape and fauna around them. For example, the well-documented acceleration of extinctions by humans today is mirrored in smaller measure in our prehistoric days, when humans are believed to have exterminated the Ice Age mammals. As documented by G.P. Marsh in *Man and Nature*, the Mediterranean world was changed drastically in classical times, converting much fertile soil and forest to desert. Furthermore, purely natural events that create devastation and waste tend to be infrequent, and the resulting conditions usually allow for natural restoration in a reasonable time. This is not usually the case with human waste and destruction, which produce toxic or incompatible conditions for natural regrowth, such as landfills with materials that won't degrade for five hundred years.

Certainly, the production of waste and the waste of resources have accelerated greatly in modern times as a result of industrialization, urbanization, and (ironically) the rise of technology. Native, so-called "primitive" cultures generally husband their resources more than modern societies because their means for extracting them are so much more limited; having less input of material results inevitably in less waste. Once human populations reach a certain scale, whether now or in ancient times, they struggle to manage whatever waste is produced because it can no longer easily be assimilated in nature. Add to this density problem the production of new materials, products, and packaging in modern societies, and waste becomes multiplied exponentially over traditional levels regardless of the country or culture. Mountainous dumps are common outside all metropolitan areas in both developed and developing countries, and the throw-away practices of modern economies infiltrate inexorably even into the latter. Should one doubt the magnitude of waste involved, simply refer to recent reports of the tens of thousands of tons of waste produced each day in megalopolises around the world.

Against this prevailing ethos of waste and consumption there are countervailing trends in modern society to minimize waste. Recycling has certainly helped to some extent, but it is still limited overall in how much waste it can reduce, as production processes as well as products and services themselves must be redesigned to reduce waste throughout the life-cycle. Reducing consumption to begin with reduces the quantity of throughput and waste. Unfortunately, consumers do not respond to appeals to reduce consumption, particularly because the system is geared to stoke it and economic growth measured by it. Moreover, those in developing countries with much less to start with do not want to be prevented from improving their standard of living, which aligns closely with the possession of goods and services.

Nonetheless, a few hardy souls have banded together to fight all this waste: a colleague has formed an online group for those who "hate" waste to share information and stories. I feel kinship with these people, as I fight a daily battle against all the waste around me at home and outside. Whether it's turning off the lights when leaving a room (not to waste electricity) or using all of a product like toothpaste or a pencil (not to waste resources), mindful waste-watchers will find that others are oblivious to what pains them constantly. When they speak out (to family or friends) against wasteful practices., they may be surprised by the response, as when my (grown) son retorted that the little I save turning off the lights was infinitesimal compared to overall use and therefore not worth considering. Pointing out the multiplier effect if everyone changed their habits was of little use, as it was clear to him this wouldn't happen anytime soon.

What, then, is this all about? Certainly, ignorance and disregard for the effects of waste underlie our wasteful practices. Society separates us from both the resources we extract and the waste we produce: paper comes from the store, and garbage goes out the door in a bag or can. Few see or think about the forests that are cut or the landfills that build up and often leak around us. This leads to an attitude of indifference. Only when we are forced to "pay" for the garbage through tipping fees or limited collections, or to recycle by mandatory policies, do we alter our habits. The ease of disposal in urban areas also provides little incentive to reduce waste; rural dwellers responsible for hauling their waste to the town dump may be more sensitive to the sheer quantities they produce.

Behind the indifference may also lurk arrogance, that we are entitled to use all the resources we consume and can therefore disregard the waste that may result. Until we started facing shortages in the twentieth century, our prevailing attitude was a lack of inhibition about exploiting natural resources. This was backed by Western religious rationalizations derived from humanity's place at the top of the biological pecking order; husbandry and stewardship, also technically part of this religious teaching, figured much less prominently. And so, in the New World, just as much earlier in the ancient one, we virtually razed the New England landscape for pasturage and crops; clear-cut the abundant hardwood forests of the upper Midwest for lumber and to make charcoal for iron processing; and nearly decimated wading birds for their plumage for millinery. Other instances of our arrogant, senseless decimation include the wanton slaughter of buffalo from trains and the mass slaughter leading to extinction of passenger pigeons for sport.

Programs to create and protect parks and forested lands emerged in the late nineteenth and early twentieth centuries, but consumption of natural resources and production of domestic and industrial waste continued apace in the rest of the U.S. With growing awareness of the effects of urbanization and industrialization, additional laws later in the twentieth century sought to limit the most harmful types of waste (i.e., pollution), such as through the Clean Air and Clean Water Acts and the hazardous waste law (RCRA), as well as our impacts on other species and their habitats, primarily through the Endangered Species Act. Recurring attacks on the ESA since its passage in 1973 demonstrate, however, that concern for other species and the resources they require is not paramount in many people's minds compared to the primacy of human needs. In fact, humans now consume more natural resources each year than the Earth replenishes. The sense of mastery over nature thus fuels our continued excessive use of resources and production of enormous quantities of waste.

The contrarian might argue that in order to progress materially, society must consume at an aggressive pace and technology be allowed to develop, even if waste inevitably results. Opponents of stringent laws to protect natural resources and the environment often argue that they limit the economic growth necessary to bring all of society to a reasonable material level. One might argue about the material level necessary for living comfortably today, but the more germane question here is whether any modern, developed society requires waste as a necessary by-product. The answer is yes and no. Today, with the technologies immediately available, we do not have the ability to reuse or recycle everything we use, nor to consume only what we really need. Progress is being made along the former lines with design for the environment, industrial ecology, and the like, but we still hit a wall at about 70% for recycling of municipal solid waste. We also continue to struggle with energy inefficiency in transportation, domestic, and industrial applications, although all three have seen significant improvements over recent decades. In the production and consumption of food, recent studies show that about 40% of food winds up wasted under current systems.

But waste is not necessary to make society more developed and materially comfortable if we applied the proper attitude and technologies from the beginning. After all, the same sense of limits and husbandry that "primitive" cultures have toward their resources could be incorporated throughout more "advanced" technological societies. Arguably, these "inhibitions" would not hold us back from development and might even save us much time as well as resources, as we wouldn't have to backtrack to clean up the mess and poisoning we created. It may be pointless to argue thus about the past,[6] but it suggests a way forward that could drastically lessen our waste.

On the individual side, is it also too inhibiting to ask people to limit their waste as they conduct their lives? Is it psychologically limiting to human growth, leading to self-abnegation and denial? Some of us who are very conscious of reducing waste do, after all, go to extremes that might border on neuroses (disclosure and true confession: I use pencils down to the end and paper all over the margins). But one must ask whether these are a reaction to the excessive waste all around and would not otherwise be manifested in a less wasteful society. For most of us, waste and destruction should not be a necessary part of our activities. Again, a small amount of attention paid to such matters ahead and during a process can save a large amount later in compensation or regret.

We come finally to the question of a solution. Is there any hope for solving our waste? And, if so, what form is a solution likely to take? Of course, there is hope: the progress we have made in reducing waste (if not consumption) through recycling and better design of products and production processes indicates that it is possible, both humanly and technically. Whether society can become totally self-sufficient from a resource perspective is not clear, but with a lot of work, we can hopefully come within the limits of Earth's renewable resources. After all, this is not just a hope, but a necessity for us to survive in the long term.

The particular solutions to achieve this state have been well delineated over recent decades with the development of the green economy, industrial ecology, net-zero energy, and the like. The more challenging issue is getting society to embrace these approaches. Government has a critical role to foster and enforce these approaches, while industry and individuals will follow suit as

---

[6] It would, for example, be inappropriate to criticize the pioneers, who faced a difficult wilderness and uncertain survival, for their use of the land and resources in North America. But this could apply to the industrialists and others who followed them later and over-exploited the land and resources.

economics inevitably incorporates the additional cost of waste and excess consumption (as resources become increasingly scarce). The attitude of the individual – going back to the sense of mastery and entitlement – may be hardest to change. Yet, economic and financial incentives will also make less wasteful practices more attractive and create a virtuous circle that, over time, should change attitudes toward waste and consumption. What was once considered a necessary corollary to material improvement will eventually be seen as detrimental and a sign of wasteful inefficiency.

Time is on our side here, but only if we embrace necessary change. That means pushing back on efforts to maintain the wasteful status quo; educating cheerfully; and, most importantly, building into the economy the means to reuse all possible resources and minimize the consumption of additional resources. Eventually, we will all revel in the clean economy these actions produce. It will be a "house" that is comfortable for us to live in again.

Charitable Treachery

WHAT IS IT ABOUT charitable organizations, including non-profit groups and educational institutions, that causes people in them to behave more disagreeably than business people competing for profit?

The oft-quoted witticism, "Academic politics are so vicious because the stakes are so small," addresses this paradox but does not really explain it. Why, after all, would people behave viciously toward each other if there is so little at stake? It may be insinuated that academics are small-minded, mean-spirited people who gravitate to an institution that allows for such behavior without its causing harm to the rest of society. Alternatively, while the faculty and staff may truly be high-minded, the issues they decide have little real consequence to society and their lofty intentions clash over matters they perceive as more important than they are.

A similar charge might be leveled at non-profit organizations, so-called charities, which are formed specifically to solve real problems in society. For while the issues charities deal with are significant, the actual influence they have on them seldom matches the charities' ambitious goals. Yet staff and board members typically have the most serious intentions to help the world, and disagreements within and between organizations can get nasty. They argue over the best way to achieve a shared goal or over which goal to pursue first. They clash over whom to befriend and whom to oppose and whether to take a hard or soft stance on a looming issue. As in politics, they disagree over the wisdom of engaging the other side constructively, and extreme partisans may even charge moderates with being complicit with the opposing side.

For the staffs of non-profit organizations, the discrepancy between these lofty goals and their inability to achieve them can cause intense frustration and unproductive friction. Most non-profits, especially smaller ones, are chronically underfunded and understaffed, and so they don't have the resources to do more than a portion of their desired programs. In addition, non-profits are not usually in a position to control the events they wish to shape. This is not to say they cannot have a significant influence on policy and practice, but that it must be achieved through persuasion or pressure. In the final analysis, someone else, typically government or business, has decision-making power that determines the outcome of an issue.

In addition to this legitimate frustration that causes friction among non-profit staff, there are always individuals who promote worthy causes in an overly aggressive way. They may be so passionate about the issues that they walk over other people who get in the way of their setting things right. They may be egotistical people who use righteous causes for personal aggrandizement. Or they may be ill-behaved people who never learned how to work with others constructively. All these types may, of course, be found in any organization or group endeavor, including business. When placed in a non-profit setting, however, the zealous, egotistical, and ill-behaved types can disguise these traits with the worthy causes they champion, giving them more license than they have in a constrained business environment.

Non-profit boards of directors are another matter. They, too, can get unpleasant in their disagreements about the direction and control of organizations, for which they have ultimate responsibility. Yet, boards are always removed from the operations of their organizations, and non-profit boards are typically so removed that they often know little about them. For non-profit boards almost always serve on a voluntary basis without compensation. The volunteers may believe strongly in their organizations' goals, or they may just want to pad their resumes. Often, particularly with larger, more prestigious non-profits, boards are comprised mostly of wealthy, well-connected individuals, and they invite onto the boards others of a similar kind who want to be with their friends.

Regrettably, most non-profit board members do not understand how to fulfill their function. Their primary roles are to set the overall direction for an organization and maintain the integrity of its operations and finances. Instead, if they get involved at all, board members may mistake their function as executive in nature and want to tell staff how to do their jobs. Some board members try to run the organization, and an individual board member may even seek to be its chief executive officer. With all this confusion of roles and responsibilities and no real referee involved,[7] non-profit boards can be ugly free-for-alls of clashing views and personalities.

A close companion to non-profit boards are the charitable foundations that support them. These are founded by very wealthy individuals and influential people, typically with a particular orientation regarding social matters they choose to address. Their professional staffs can be helpful to non-profit leaders, but too often they wield their derivative power over non-profits, rejecting their proposals dismissively or pushing them in their preferred directions. Foundations tend to move like cattle, trending with particular issues they want to fund and ignoring others. With the limited money at stake, the righteous causes involved, and the naked displays of

---

[7] Unlike for-profit companies, non-profit organizations do not have shareholders watching over the board. The only recourse is the attorney-general of the state in which a non-profit is incorporated, but appealing at this level is a high bar.

personal power, foundations can add to the unpleasantness of life in the charitable world.

It may be painfully apparent that the writer has experience in the non-profit world. I came to believe that most of my colleagues in the business world, with whom I often disagreed over goals or means, were more trustworthy and collegial than many peers in similar non-profits as mine. It does not help, of course, that non-profits have to compete with one another for attention in the media or before government and business groups they wish to influence. Nor that all of us are in a big gladiator arena vying for limited funds from grant-giving foundations and agencies.

I should hasten to add, however, that I would not have stayed in the non-profit arena as long as I did if it didn't have excellent people who truly want to achieve socially important goals and have the maturity to work toward them in a cooperative way. I also had the privilege to serve a long time under a chairperson and board that understood their role in non-profit governance and opened many doors for our programs without interfering with our operations.

Educational institutions mirror many of the issues of non-profit organizations but have their own peculiarities. Unlike charities, they are not generally oriented to solutions of societal problems in a hands-on sense, although that has changed somewhat over the years. Traditionally, academe studies subject areas and issues to improve our understanding of them, researching them in ways activists have no time or inclination to do. The very walls (ivy-covered) of higher education symbolize a tranquility and separation from the hustle-bustle of daily life. Researchers are expected to take a more objective, longer-term view of problems in order to get at the root of them. Subject areas with no practical or immediate application to contemporary society are also fostered in this environment.

This detachment explains the limited import of many issues disputed in the academic world. Among researchers there are always differences of opinion about key aspects of their fields; in most cases these are arcane and, well, academic. Among educational theorists there are continual disagreements about the best ways to educate students. Among faculty and administrators, disputes about internal matters have little relevance to the outside except when issues relate to larger societal ones, such as a university's investment in objectionable activities (such as apartheid). Generally, though, what goes on behind the ivy walls does not arouse attention outside them. Hence the charge that academic politics gets heated over inconsequential matters.

But is the academic world truly more vicious than the business world? Certainly, business can be ruthless as companies vie for sales, market share, and innovations that will beat out competitors. Profit has never been known to moderate greed or inspire good behavior. Industry in the United States has a history of trampling on competitors and others who may impede its goals. Regulations to control these behaviors fill many volumes, and scarcely a month goes by without news of their infringement by a company.

The question, though, is not about bad corporate behavior alone but whether personal animosity accompanies it. While examples do exist of bad blood in the business world, even between large corporations, that kind of negativity is not generally characteristic of business competition, which is an accepted principle of the market. Competition is an omnipresent aspect of higher education, too, as faculty compete for tenured positions, research grants, and coveted awards and perquisites. But in academe the competition is almost always on an individual basis, allowing the more aggressive, egotistical, and ill-behaved to undermine with virtual impunity others who threaten them. In contrast, businesses are generally operated by groups, and it is more difficult for someone to take such personal action against someone else. Sabotaging others does, of course, happen within a company – human nature does not vary much – but can be controlled by management setting the right tone and not rewarding such behavior with the advancement it seeks.

What ultimately makes bad behavior in the charitable world so disappointing is the contrast between such behavior and the lofty goals of charitable work. One might least expect to see back-stabbers in a non-profit group intended for social benefit or a university dedicated to truth. But with strong ambitions, large frustrations, and a detachment from society at large, those who work in these institutions can turn treacherously on one another in unpleasant and unbecoming ways.

Personalities

WHAT IS IT ABOUT personalities that makes them instantly likable or not? How can personality show through our face so transparently and in such variety, and why does it do so?

We've all met persons whose friendly visage and posture makes us want to know them from the start. They effuse warmth from their eyes, and their words and smiles typically reinforce the welcome. There are cooler people who avert their glance and avoid committing either way toward us. And then there are hard people, who look challengingly at or through us with stone-cold eyes and who spurn social niceties to take the upper hand. Among the latter one may confront a truly malevolent person whose inner evil radiates out in an unmistakable and frightful way.

Of course, there are actually many more personality types and first impressions one may get from a person's bearing. Some may not fit neatly into a "good-neutral-hard" categorization but may vary instead from engaged to detached. An initial response from someone may not truly reflect their nature or attitude toward others. We have all experienced meeting someone who seemed reserved but who subsequently warmed up to us, perhaps becoming a good friend. We have also met people whose initial good impression did not hold up as we got to know them better. Personalities can act like an onion, with different layers manifesting themselves as the occasion or time warrants.

But in many ways people do broadcast their attitude to the world as they carry on in public and meet others. Facial expressions and body language can be revealing, often beyond what people consciously realize. Some of us scowl, others beam, while most carry on indifferently to others. We read these non-verbal signs because they are a clue how to deal with someone and what to expect in the future. In primitive times these signs were likely crucial to our survival. Our gut is designed to interpret them automatically by sizing up the gestalt of a person's bearing and intent. That is why someone may immediately appeal to us or not. Of course, our gut is not always correct, and we may be fooled by someone dissembling a friendly demeanor. This can cause harm subsequently and make us more cautious before opening up to someone again.

Our body – primarily, our face – can be a window into our personalities. It is true that many people function in a neutral or indifferent manner, exhibiting nothing too positive or negative to those around them. But this, too, can be revealing as to personality: the expressionless face suggests the person is either internally occupied or slightly wary of their surroundings. It is possibly a readiness mode or an insular one – seemingly contradictory, but not necessarily. In contrast, smiley faces in public convey a generally positive emotion to others. They can represent true good will that shines through – to which we instantly react positively – or a more formal courtesy toward others. The latter expression usually appears more strained, more set than the former, and our gut may caution that not all is so friendly underneath.

The hard and malevolent types reveal themselves through their eyes, brows, and mouths, with postures in support. The furrowing and squinting of the eyes help make them look hard and unsympathetic toward others, but there is an additional quality of heartlessness in the eyes that can be truly disturbing. The body can be neutral or menacing in turn, with hunched up shoulders or inappropriate distance from others. No doubt some who demonstrate such attributes do so defensively and may be more decent underneath, but one wonders what compels the negative stance. One summer when I was adding air to my car's tires at a gas station, a man came up to do the same and stood practically over me with a glare. Was he in a hurry to get home from vacation, or just an obnoxious, malevolent type used to bullying his way? It didn't matter to me – I anticipated no additional relation to him – because the action itself was offensive.

There is always the danger we will misinterpret the negative personality just as we might the positive one. With the former we may be susceptible to projecting our own fears or negativity on someone else's appearance. We may interpret a neutral or guarded attitude as hard or malevolent. This won't usually have negative consequences unless we blatantly act on the reading. Nevertheless, the malevolence of some people seems unmistakable. I have crossed paths in city sidewalks with a few people whose glower could not have been more clear and ill-intended.

It is also a wonder how our face can transmit so much information about personality and in such variety. The three basic personality categories are simplifications of what people actually show. Personality attributes like honesty, sympathy, tact, crudeness, rudeness, introversion, extraversion, generosity, selfishness, and so on can all show through a person's face and body language. Portrait artists and caricaturists know how to portray these traits through subtle features of the eyes, mouth, nose, and facial muscles. Novelists convey these characteristics through words describing these features. The rest of us are more-or-less adept at reading these signs based on perception and experience.

It remains to understand how the mind expresses this information through the body, and why. The process by which our emotions express themselves through our facial muscles appears to be an outing of sorts, a necessary venting of what we feel inside that would otherwise be repressed. If we try not smiling when we see a good friend or not scowling when we are angry, we can see just how strong the signal is that our mind sends to our face to express our feelings. Attitudes such as condescension or disgust can have the same power to reveal themselves despite efforts to conceal them. Some traits and emotions also involve body posture, while others are so strong (like bullying or rage) that the body takes over.

Why the mind would reveal itself so transparently this way is less clear. From an evolutionary perspective it is vital for us to read others' intent, but it would seem equally important for us to conceal our own or at least control its expression to others. Yet most of us do not have a good "poker face" to do this. We can't help showing what we feel in most situations, whether mirth that bursts out inappropriately or disdain we can't withhold. Those who keep their emotions "under wraps" are exceptions and noted as such. I had a school teacher whose anger at bad behavior was expressed in quiet commands and expressionless stares; he was feared more than any other. For such people seem to have the upper hand by not showing theirs.

Perhaps expression of our personalities and emotions through our bodies is part of the social compact. Imagine if everyone acted like this teacher: people would never know where they stood with respect to others, whether friend or foe. The withheld personality may be a relic of the earliest days, when everyone was potentially an adversary and nothing could be revealed until proven safe to do so. Once people began to live together in larger social groups, facial signs became an expected form of communication. Naturally, personality became untethered as well and found free expression in the face. So now, in today's societies, we can read each other's natures to some extent without saying a word.

Intentionally Blank

WHAT IS IT ABOUT ignorance that makes us willfully want to perpetuate it? Does our intentional ignorance help us or harm us from an evolutionary perspective?

To start with the premise, putting it another way, most of us have limited curiosity about the world, particularly its more intricate aspects. We are too willing to shrug off information that challenges our comprehension, either leaving it for experts or implying that it isn't that important for our lives. We may even disparage those who relish such information and understand it. The disparity between those few and the rest is most stark in the school years, where the knowledgeable are labeled as "nerds" or "wonks" and often mocked. As people mature, the difference manifests itself in terms of professions and occupations, social classes, and even geographic areas. Here the gap in knowledge is implicit, and the condescension of the learned and the resentment of the less informed are largely latent. Politicians often exploit the resentment by branding the informed as elites, suggesting they are not superior but merely privileged and self-serving.

The question may then be whether it is truly ignorance that differentiates us, or the type of knowledge people have depending on class, occupation, or place. Certainly, there are significant distinctions between, for example, academic versus experiential knowledge, urban versus rural know-how, and trades versus professions. Each group in these pairs tends to devalue the knowledge base of the other or consider it out of its sphere of understanding or concern. So the premise appears to hold, in that an entire viewpoint on the world is considered irrelevant to an individual in one group compared to the other.

There is also a difference between knowledge used for a genuine purpose and information used to make others look ignorant and inferior. People naturally react in the latter case by dismissing both the information and the arrogant person applying it in this way. But this leaves them vulnerable to appearing incurious as well as ignorant, fulfilling the purpose of the belittler. Those who have special knowledge should be willing to communicate it in a way that their audience can understand, or at least not make a show of superiority. Learning is never facilitated by shame or denigration.

In truth, there is so much information and knowledge about the world that no one can possibly grasp more than a very small part of it. The explosion of knowledge, particularly in scientific areas, has been well documented; the concern here is its effect on people. Much of this information is genuinely difficult to understand, and one typically has to spend years in a technical or scientific field to be conversant with it. For the vast majority who do not, the information remains opaque, esoteric, like a secret cult from which they are excluded. Attempts to understand such information usually result in frustration, hence the casual dismissal of the entire topic. Virtually all of us have confronted this wall at some point, often early in life in school with respect to certain subjects we couldn't fathom, and when no one helps open the door we come to dismiss all that's behind it and move elsewhere.

The amount of information and its complexity and apparent incomprehensibility lead to a kind of stratification of humans. In school there are the nerds and wonks versus the rest of the students. In the work world there is a host of "specialists," who deal with the vast span of knowledge and limited scope of human intelligence by carving out a piece about which they can become fully knowledgeable and conversant. Specialists may not be more intelligent than the mass of humans, but they function well in the limited area in which they work. Our society has, of course, become awash in specialists of all types. Typically we deal with all the information we cannot understand by relying on specialists, as do specialists themselves in areas outside their expertise.

People cope with this sea of incomprehensibility all around us in various ways. Some try to understand as much as possible, feeding their curiosity and handling the inevitable frustration. Others devalue much specialized knowledge and what is beyond the grasp of their everyday lives in a kind of reverse snobbery. Most people have a comfort zone that includes what they know and understand and don't pay much attention to what is outside it. You could call the second and third responses willful ignorance, because people intentionally set up a boundary between what they do know and what they don't. The term may be unfairly pejorative in that the boundary may not be of their own making, but I believe the attitude involved, while understandable, is not particularly constructive.

This general attitude of willful ignorance may nevertheless be an apt response to a bewildering world from an evolutionary perspective and may not harm the prospects of the human species overall. It certainly makes life more livable for most people, freeing them of concern for all they do not know and from feeling inferior and overwhelmed. The alternative could be debilitating, even paralyzing. Humans react to not knowing what they don't know by assuming they know all they need to know; without this presumption, they would not have the confidence to do many things.

In fact, it is just the few explorers in the human species (perhaps in all species?) who forge new paths to discover and understand new information. They are sometimes vilified by society because they reveal potentially frightening aspects of the world and shake up received notions of it. Yet their efforts can ultimately improve the survival of the species by increasing our understanding of the world. The rest of society eventually catches up, at least to some degree, while maintaining the boundary where the new knowledge gets too complex to understand for most people. Thus, for example, people accept the use of electricity in their daily lives, but few truly understand what it is, how it works, or how it is generated.

In short, it is fully justified for most people to be "ignorant" about large parts of the world because of its complexity and difficulty. What is not so constructive is the "willful" aspect of this ignorance, either in its aggressive (devaluing) or passive (comfort zone) form. The aggressive response can lead to antagonism toward others; the passive, to complacency. And while society may still progress thanks to the few whose curiosity and energy lead them to explore the unknown and the complex known, we would likely be a more interesting and caring people if we all cared more about more of the world around us.

Anthropocentric

WHAT IS IT ABOUT human beings, that virtually everything must be in reference to ourselves? Is this unnatural, and does it have consequences for ourselves and other species?

We need look only at our literature, which reflects society's values and concerns: we write endlessly about ourselves and our view of the world, whether in fiction or non-fiction. There is the occasional work involving a domesticated animal or a relationship to a wild one (most famously, *Moby Dick*), but rare is the work devoted solely to animals from their perspective. In fact, I can think of only one, Salten's novel *Bambi*, that is not exclusively children's literature, which always uses animals in an anthropomorphic or romanticized way. At most, in certain authors nature is an important background or chorus on human action, perhaps equal to a character, as in Thomas Hardy's novels of human drama on the English heath. So, too, the popular literature on history, politics, religion, biographies, self-help, astrology, etc., vastly outnumbers that on nature, astronomy, etc.

While there are certainly lovers of nature and wild animals, the vast majority of people is generally indifferent to the natural world. Given a choice of watching a human subject or a typical natural one, most of us inevitably gravitate to the former. The popularity of glamorous landscapes and celebrity animals like pandas and elephants only proves the point.

Science might seem to contradict such anthropocentrism, since it (particularly biology and ecology) studies the world around us and all life forms. But this uniquely human pursuit is almost always conducted in objectified terms, that is, from the "third person" perspective, us. In fact, much science and the applications that result from it are for human use and benefit, from materials and resources to food and drugs. The scientist or naturalist who is immersed in the non-human world for its own sake is something of a rarity in the overall scheme. For this individual the objectification of science is counterbalanced by the reverence he or she usually feels toward the natural world.

Yet, our anthropocentrism is not unnatural, nor is it misguided from either an evolutionary or psychological perspective. All sentient beings see the world from their own perspective; each is at the center of its world. This is a natural response other species undoubtedly share with us in their own way, primarily for the sake of survival, but also as a direct result of the perceptual faculties of all animals. In short, it would be hard to imagine how any species or individual could survive that did not see the world first in terms of itself, its needs, and its survival. Moreover, without this "grounding" in self, an individual would be lost psychologically and would not be able to relate to the world around it.

The problem of anthropocentrism arises with humans, however, because of the enormity of our impact on the rest of the world. Unlike any other earthly species, we have the capacity to shape the world to our need and liking, transforming landscapes and ecosystems entirely. The attitude that humans are all that really counts, that other species and "resources" serve human needs primarily, has led to serious disruptions in our world and repercussions for human society. Purely from a self-centered, survival perspective, we have learned to protect the environment and conserve resources to some degree. This has not necessarily mitigated our anthropocentrism, as the focus remains on our needs, but it has provided an avenue for some humans to see the world from a different perspective.

For while humans are animals who need to take care of themselves, we also have a special capability to transcend the psychological limitations that likely pertain to all other animal species.[8] That is a sense of value beyond our self, of a moral obligation to care for the world beyond our immediate circle of concern (self, family, neighbors, town, affinity groups, nation, etc.). Ultimately, this means caring for other species and for the world at large – not just because we need them for our survival, but for the sake of all species' survival and for the integrity of the environment itself.[9]

With this special capability – a moral sense of concern for the world – humans can both provide for themselves and also ensure the well-being of other species and their habitats. Anthropocentrists can become anthropo-stewards. This concept has arisen in modern ecological thought, even tying it to ancient Biblical directives. But the critical point in a moral philosophy of nature is that our stewardship should not solely be determined by human needs.

---

[8] That all other animals share the same level of species-centrism is conjectural, although reasonable in terms of what we experience with other species and their shared survival needs. Many animal species are highly intelligent and display intricate social structures, the capacity for altruism (even across species), and caring for one another. Hence, we cannot be sure that all animals of higher intelligence see the world in their own centric terms alone.

[9] This thesis is amplified in my book, *In the Light of Humane Nature*, 2014.

We are certainly far from realizing this high level of moral concern. In most people's thinking, as well as in the national culture, nature is still seen primarily as a resource to be used for human purposes. The advances made in national and international environmental policy both reflect this limitation and offer hope for a broader, more stewardship-like view. The initial acts of conservation in nineteenth-century America were driven by rampant waste of resources and concern that we would run out of timber (hence, creation of national forests) and scenic areas (hence, creation of national parks). Not until the twentieth century and passage of such laws as the Endangered Species Act and Wilderness Act did a more ecological view of nature begin to be set in national policy. Even then, preservation of other species and of natural land had to be tied back to values "to the Nation and its people" and "use and enjoyment of the American people," respectively. But purely commercial or economic uses of the land and other species were no longer the sole determining factor.

So far in this discussion, anthropocentrism has been described as a natural, instinctive response of the human species to its survival needs, comparable to how all other species presumably react to life. There is another, more pernicious connotation of anthropocentrism that needs to be addressed: the belief that humans are the most significant entity in the universe and are entitled to exploit the Earth. This "hard" anthropocentrism is defined more fully as follows (*Encyclopaedia Britannica* on-line):

> Anthropocentrism, philosophical viewpoint arguing that human beings are the central or most significant entities in the world. This is a basic belief embedded in many Western religions and philosophies. Anthropocentrism regards humans as separate from and superior to nature and holds that human life has intrinsic value while other entities (including animals, plants, mineral resources, and so on) are resources that may justifiably be exploited for the benefit of humankind.

Let's focus on several key words and phrases here: "most significant entities," "separate," "superior," "intrinsic value," "exploited." Clearly, there are religious sects that adhere to these beliefs, and there is no point in arguing with them. From a philosophical and ecological point-of-view, however, it is easy to take exception to most of these claims.

Humans are certainly the most significant entities to ourselves, but it is difficult to see how significance can be ascribed to us in any universal sense other than our impact on the world. In that regard, it is our very sense of being separate from and supposedly superior to nature that has caused us to destroy so much of nature, even our own life-support in many cases (e.g., deforestation and desertification, climate change, stratospheric ozone depletion, air and water pollution, pervasive toxic pollution, invasive species, species and habitat loss, etc.). Whenever humans have put themselves apart from nature and its immutable laws, we get whip-sawed by her (example: coastal development and consequent flooding from storms). Our sense of superiority because of our advanced intelligence also gets humbled regularly by all that we don't know about how the world works (example: climate change from greenhouse gas emissions). Moreover, an argument has been made that by separating ourselves from nature, we have lost our roots and an important part of our spiritual grounding.

As to our intrinsic value, like significance, there is no reference point for this claim. What is it that is intrinsically valuable and to whom, other than ourselves? Are not all species intrinsically valuable to themselves? I would, in fact, argue for the intrinsic value of all species and all life, but that is not exclusive to humans. And so, the entitlement that exclusively human value would give us to exploit all other species and Earth resources is false. How, indeed, could any humane view of the world justify exploitation, and for only one species's benefit, at that?

Arguably, in the matter of conceptual, technical, and linguistic intelligence, the human species has attained a significant level of superiority over all other animal species. This has led us to create modes of sheltering and feeding ourselves that depart significantly from all other species, and to develop a vast culture as we transcended mere survival mode. These are true human achievements that appear to be unique to our species. Our languages, our arts and sciences, our cultures and institutions, and our technologies set us apart from the rest. But they do not *ipso facto* entitle us to rule over and exploit all other creatures on Earth. Instead, the (apparently) uniquely moral sense that human culture has also developed should direct us to have an appreciative and protective attitude toward our fellow species on Earth. Paradoxically, this moral potential, not fully realized in most individuals and society, ultimately suggests we do what no other species does – to consider all other species almost equally to our own.

Releasing ourselves from both the hard anthropocentrism and the more natural type, which also has negative consequences, could only broaden our vision and awareness of the world. We will continue to write about ourselves, but will give much more consideration to the rest of the world and other species, beyond the limited naturalist books and movies of today. We will continue to explore the universe beyond our planet, but give rightful place to learning more about our planet itself. We know so little about the Earth and its inhabitants. We have only rudimentary knowledge about the social structure of many animals, their ways of congregating and communicating, and their life-cycles. Besides knowing more about our fellow creatures, we could learn valuable lessons from our brethren in all these areas. We are a relatively young species, and others have learned through evolution, intelligence, and adaptation how to get along in this world of change. Just as ontology repeats phylogeny, we can discern stages of development in other species that give insight into our own. We can also, non-anthropocentrically, learn to appreciate other species more for what they are.

In the ultimate expansion, our literature may include fiction about other species from their own perspective. It would portray animals in their natural settings and, based on knowledge of the species, create action using their natural behaviors. It may, for example, tell of the evolution of an animal (or even plant) community with the same fictional devices we use for human stories. It may center on a few individuals and their (appropriate and characteristic) acts, eschewing anthropomorphic versions that have hitherto characterized such efforts. Interaction with humans could be included, but they are not the point-of-view from which the story is told.

Of course, I realize the irony of humans creating a literature meant to focus on non-humans. To the best of our knowledge, literature is exclusively a human enterprise. What this new genre represents is, like moral behavior, an effort by us to get outside our skin, to see the world from a broader perspective, which is quite due from an historical and developmental view. It would produce many more works like *Bambi*, but without its then inevitable anthropomorphism and, perhaps, with no longer a need for its misanthropy.

Doing It Right Daily

WHAT IS IT ABOUT daily tasks and routines that makes them so difficult to do right, and how should they best be done?

To approach this topic fully informed, the reader is encouraged to peruse the companion essay, "Every Day," which discusses the variation in people's daily tasks and routines and how they go about doing them. Our subject here concerns the tasks and routines themselves and how they can best be performed. For, like many aspects of life, daily tasks and routines are more difficult to do properly than they appear.

Perhaps the reader feels uneasy with the suggestion that there is a "right" way to conduct one's personal tasks. It may come as a shock to some that Momma's advice wasn't always the best. But just forget who taught you how to do things in a faulty way, and you won't be defensive about relinquishing them. It's not just for marketing purposes and profit that great corporations like Procter & Gamble and Unilever spend millions developing innovative new products and applications to clean our bodies and houses. We really do need all this commercial help to do right what our forebears did more simply and ignorantly.

Personal hygiene became more difficult once humans decided to leave the savannah and live in cities, as they forsook all their natural habits. Technology made normal human functions more complicated and sometimes counterintuitive, like bringing inside what properly belonged in the woods. Of course, such senseless shifts required wholesale changes in protocol, which few have mastered even to this day. The very unmentionable quality of these tasks also made instruction about them nearly impossible, perpetuating bad habits and unspeakable results.

As for proper dress and cleanliness, the difficulties involved vary by gender. Men are mostly clueless about these matters and deal with them randomly each day. They sometimes get things right by serendipity, but usually they have to try several times not to put their undershirt on inside-out or squirt the shaving cream on the floor. While women are quite savvy in their dress and care, these have become so complicated that prolonged instruction and practice are required to produce the desired result. The average woman – not even a fashionista – must devote significant time to mastering the relevant products on the market.

Housekeeping techniques have always been a challenge to civilized humans. Somewhat like the unmentionables, life became more complicated when we forsook the outside for an interior existence. It was so much easier to clean the bedroom when we lived in trees and let rain sweep away the dust bunnies underneath. So, too, cleaning up the dishes when we didn't use any. Nowadays, entire industries are built around cleaning up kitchen and bathroom waste inside our houses rather than letting natural degradation consume them.

In summary, our civilization has created the difficulties we all face in properly executing our daily personal and housekeeping tasks. Technology has, as in most cases, outpaced the wits of most humans to embrace it. The reader will therefore be grateful that this essay intends to right the imbalance by providing sage advice on how to do things right.

Forsaking delicacy and in full disclosure of my own deficient upbringing, we'll start with some unmentionables. I had to learn from a college roommate how to spool out bathroom tissue (aka toilet paper) on my hand so it wouldn't rub me roughly when used. To wit, fold it back-and-forth by the squares perforated on the roll – don't just crumple it up into a twisted mass. Although the folding technique may seem superfluous for such a lowly task, it prevents unwanted vibrations from reaching the brain. Likewise, applying new deodorant over old, while unavoidable when camping, can cause chemical reactions not anticipated by manufacturers and toxic shock to your clothes. Be sure to wash under the arms first in the morning.

Dental hygiene is a challenge for all, and I have several tips to offer, having had to become an amateur hygienist to retain my chops. We learned in childhood to brush back-and-forth, maybe up-and-down occasionally. Wrong! The proper brush stroke is rotary, as teeth and gums take umbrage at being pushed around. For while teeth may appear to be linear, they are full of curves and indentations, which only rotary action can clean. Of course, if you use one of the newfangled rotary toothbrushes, don't make the mistake of applying it in circles, as this will thoroughly confuse your mouth and may cause vortices in your tooth pulp in the worst cases. As for flossing, the biggest step is doing it, and more than just for the first time. If you do, you must aim so that the little bits of food come popping out at the mirror in front of you. If they hit inside your mouth, you'll have to floss all over again, most likely.

Showering seems like such a simple task, but once again, there is a *right* way to do it versus the way everyone actually does it. For some reason people think that once the shower gets turned on, it must stay on for the duration of their ablutions. They look quizzically at the little rod at the top of the shower head and wonder why it causes the shower to drip when pushed in. I'll forbear the environmental lecture here only to wonder how people can soap up when water is blowing all over them. An additional tip is to start washing from the top and move down, as this may obviate the need to wash the lower half of your body.

At the other end of the day, undressing for bedtime, it is essential to lay out one's underwear to air before throwing it in the laundry. And yes, it should stay out for the entire night. While this may offend your spouse or roommate, the benefit more than compensates for the rift it may cause in your relationships. For as your underwear emits vapors to the bedroom, it allows you to reconnect with parts of yourself you ignored during the day. This therefore qualifies as one of the best holistic techniques available, and cheap to boot. I am certain I am the only person who does this and am therefore pleased to provide this technique to the public for its benefit.

Housekeeping challenges are greatest in the bathrooms and kitchen. For the former, the solution is quite clear: wait for the maids. This will build character owing to the disgust it causes in the meantime. The strategy will not, unfortunately, work for the kitchen, as dishes and pots piling up soon obstruct all attempts at self-feeding. My solution has been to use rubber gloves to wash the pots, since this makes me think someone else is doing the work. The dishes can mostly be loaded into the dishwasher (which I hope you have), and herein lies a near treatise on proper techniques. Like the approach to daily routines as a whole (see companion essay), the loading of a dishwasher divides along a distinct cleavage of personality types. One group, benighted I must say, simply piles dishes in haphazardly at every angle, with the sorry result that half of them stay soiled because the water doesn't reach them or the rotor underneath is obstructed. The other group, anal-retentive though it be, properly puts each dish upright in its slot, avoiding any contact with others, in keeping with the person's antisocial disposition.

Now, the reader may suspect that some of these techniques are fishy, or at least the rationales for them are. Let me assure you that I have personally tried out all these techniques, which have been honed over the years to near perfection for the benefits so designated. I have wondered why no one before me has offered this kind of homely advice. Perhaps it has been out of excessive homage to one's parents, who should have provided proper guidance on daily tasks to begin with. This misplaced loyalty has caused generations of unkempt and unfit adults to launch into the world when they can't even get things right at home. Now, at last, we can look forward to a bright future as succeeding generations do it right daily.

Style, Fashion, and Fads

WHAT IS IT ABOUT human culture that it is so guided by style and fashion, and why are they so changeable? Is there any significance to style and fashion or any difference between them? And how do fads fit into the picture?

Style and fashion are most closely associated today with the clothing industry and how people dress. But the concepts apply more broadly to cultural expression and social mores, ranging from personal behavior to the arts. Style, in particular, has a wide array of applications: we talk of an individual's style in dress, talk, or behavior; the style of a newspaper or magazine; or the style of music, literature, art, or architecture, writ large. The latter often encompasses long periods of artistic movements, such as the Classical or Baroque styles in music and architecture.

Fashion, by contrast, tends to connote trends of shorter duration than style, although the terms are often used interchangeably. The expressions, "out of style" and "out of fashion," are essentially identical in meaning. Yet, some icons of high fashion take pains to distinguish the two, maintaining that style is a permanent feature of a person. In any case, both style and fashion are time-limited. No matter how long any style persists, it is eventually superseded by another one.

The phenomena we call style and fashion are particular, repeated patterns in whatever medium to which they are applied. A style of speech involves certain phrases or intonations or diction; of dress, a similar way of putting cloth together to cover the body (or not); of art, a way of portraying the world or human emotion and using tactile materials; and of music or architecture, a typical form or structure for presenting the material, and of the former also the particular harmonies, instruments, and emotional content of the notes. Often, especially with regard to movements, the development of a style takes place over years and only becomes recognizable in retrospect. Historians sometimes demarcate styles somewhat arbitrarily, drawing clear lines between periods when styles actually evolve and overlap as they transition from one to another. Distinctive patterns rarely spring up of their own without some foundation in what was previously used.

Thus defined, style is an inescapable and meaningful aspect of human culture. Any creative act in the broadest sense is expressed through some style, whether consciously or not. Style is certainly more apparent in the creative arts and crafts (including couture), where the artist or craftsperson deliberately puts things together for effect. Style also manifests itself in everyday situations in our speech and behavior. Cultural clashes often occur because of contrasting styles of speech or behavior that are not mutually understood or appreciated. For within a culture a particular style of communication and interaction can be considered the norm.

The question posed initially, however, concerns the temporal changes of style in any given culture. Viewed over decades and centuries, style certainly does change in most cultures. But it may be only partially true to say that style is so changeable. Besides being relative in time, the speed of change in style may be more a function of the kind of expression involved. In the arts – literature, music, art, dance, architecture, etc. – style does not usually change too quickly, perhaps on the order of decades. In popular culture, including clothing, speech, and entertainment, style may change more frequently, on the order of years or even months. Fashion, particularly of the garment kind, tends to change on the shorter side of the spectrum.

As to why style and fashion change at all, many factors come into play, some depending on the medium of expression, others involving the entire culture. Broader stylistic movements like European Classicism or Romanticism tend to express the cultural spirit of a period, what the Germans picturesquely call "Zeitgeist." Whether in music or mores, the conglomerate of social forces has an overall effect in shaping style. With historical change in these influences, such as the breakdown in Europe of the nobility and the rise of individualism, style changes concomitantly across media, evolving in this case to less formal, freer expression. Within a given medium, more specific factors may affect style, such as a groundbreaking artist or simply the exhaustion of material in a particular style.

Changes in style thus align to a large extent with cultural and historical changes. In cultures that change slowly, such as ancient Chinese and Egyptian dynasties, style tends to remain more uniform, although scholars can detect subtle variations in style, such as from early to late periods of dynasties. In Western civilization the pace of change has accelerated in the past half-millennium, especially with the industrial revolution beginning in the late eighteenth century. Consequently, styles of the arts and of social expression have turned over more rapidly in the modern era.

In fact, in the past hundred years or so, Western society has experienced numerous waves of short-lived styles and fashions that may be designated as fads. These are characterized as being short-term and followed with unwarranted zeal. If fashion is more transient than style, fads are even more transient than fashion. In addition, fads may be about the most insignificant things, but they become "au courant" or "in" with the trend-leaders of society and necessarily picked up by everyone else. It may be a stretch in many cases even to designate a fad as a fashion, much less a style, as many fads involve objects, interests, or a singular expression of speech. Others, however, may represent a particular style or fashion or be the harbinger of one.

For example, the hula hoop – that big plastic ring that revolves around one's waist by gyrating the hips – was a major fad in the 1960s. It ran its course but represented nothing else. In contrast, the diet world – eating certain things or less of everything to lose weight – has had many fads, where a particular diet (e.g., Mediterranean, Paleo, grapefruit, low carb, etc.) is taken up quickly by many. Dieting does figure in a particular kind of lifestyle in which one tries to be fit, chic, or not overweight. It also feeds literally into fashion, as most clothes are made (up until recently) for leaner physiques. Haircuts can also be the subject of fads, where a new type of cut or way of arranging the hair gets taken up quickly for a short time. Examples include the "Mohawk" or psychedelic highlighting. Some of these fads may, after their initial surge, persist as a fashion or style among a small number of adherents.

People tend to be very susceptible to fads. Unlike style and fashion, which tend to be the accepted mode of expression at a given cultural time, fads emerge quickly with an excitement that draws people toward them. Their power is based mostly on their novelty and on the trend-leaders who first adopt them. Most people go with the flow and happily join the craze, as it is like a virus in being infectious and almost irresistible. At the height of any fad people feel considerable pressure to conform by adopting the fad. But a fad also promises a new angle on daily life that can make it more interesting. The actual triviality of most fads can be disguised by the sheer number of people embracing them, conferring apparent significance.

The pace of social change certainly breeds more fads, as evolving events and attitudes provide new material for creative whims. In addition, the ease of telecommunication in contemporary society allows fads to spread quickly across geographies and cultures. Television was the big purveyor of fads in the late twentieth century, along with more traditional word-of-mouth. In the early twenty-first century the Internet has taken over, especially social media, which allows word-of-screen to be conveyed instantly to hundreds or millions of followers, depending on one's network.

Just as with style, our speech may be influenced by fads. These involve particular words, phrases, or syntax that infiltrate otherwise conventional grammar and style. Examples of recent verbal fads are the use of "like" as a kind of conjunction joining most phrases or prefacing all descriptions; "exactly" as a substitute for "yes" for every affirmation; and "thank you so much" for every appreciative response, no matter how small the matter. Unfortunately, such verbal fads tend to be used quite frequently and do not disappear quickly, although they could hardly be said to constitute a style or fashion. They truly catch on like a virus, spreading from one mouth to another, and are equally irresistible as other fads, if not more so because of the facility of using them.

I often wonder what foreign speakers of English think when they hear us speak with these verbal fads, especially "like" being peppered generously everywhere. It certainly isn't in any ESL classes, I would think. Their use suggests that even native speakers have difficulty expressing themselves verbally. Other languages have similar filler words, but I don't know if they are used quite as frequently as in English.

With style, fashion, and fads, there are those who initiate, those who follow, and those who resist. Most of us fall into the second category, following existing styles and fashions and getting caught up in some fads. To the extent style and fashion are expressions of the age, this seems appropriate, as cultural movements are usually initiated by a few creative, iconoclastic, or revolutionary individuals. These very individuals may also be ones who resist current styles and fashions because they have in mind the need for something else that is fresher or just different.

I must confess I tend to resist fads as mindless trivia distracting from the essential. But on occasion it makes me catch up when there was something to the fad. When the *Lord of the Rings* books became wildly popular – a reading fad – in the late 1960s, I resisted, only to be drawn back to reading them, with great pleasure and admiration, in the late 1970s. I missed the boat, but in this case it remained afloat for me to get on at a later date. The best styles, fashions, and even a few fads have that staying power.

Video Screens

WHAT IS IT ABOUT video screens that they can captivate us despite the mediocre content often shown on them? In what ways have they, on the other hand, significantly improved our lives?

I refer here to all the screens, large and small, inside our houses and buildings and even outside, that display moving images via television, cinema, the Internet, and closed circuits. These screens are associated with our television sets, movie theaters, computer monitors, smartphones, and waiting rooms or lobbies. In most cases nowadays, these screens emit a continuous stream of moving images on a variety of themes. Movie theaters have the greatest focus, usually displaying but one film at a time (after numerous ads and trailers).

All of these screens have the capacity to capture our attention immediately and continuously. We are drawn to a screen when we enter a room that has one, even diverting our attention from people there with whom we should engage. We can't easily look away from a screen, whether it is a television in our living room, a monitor in a public place, or a video playing on our digital toy. For this reason televisions or equivalent visual media are almost universally banned in the front of automobiles, where they could dangerously distract the driver.

How can we be more fascinated with these images on a flat, stationary surface than the three-dimensional objects and people around us? For one, the content presented is usually dynamic, moving, and variable, and this grabs our attention, probably instinctually. If the screen features a person talking, he or she usually "addresses" us directly, and we are conditioned to respond to that. If someone in the room does so as well, the competition becomes apparent and can put us in conflict, depending on the interest value of each source. A parallel situation occurs in a large conference room when the live speaker is also broadcast to the audience through monitors: even those close enough to get a good direct view often resort to the video image. This enhancement through video may be tantamount to the thrill of having one's name printed in the newspaper.

Another lure derives from the content itself. Most video displays have enough "interesting" content to keep us engaged, since that is one of their prime objectives. Whether in a program or an advertisement, the creators must not only keep the images dynamic but also maintain their interest value. Live people in a room (much less its objects) are under no such obligation. Video advertisements, known as commercials on television, have raised this allure to an art form. Big money is paid to their creators to engage potential customers, especially for programs where commercial rates are high. Some of the lures they use are obvious but perennially effective, such as beautiful scenery and people, sexual suggestion, catchy music, quick action, and even violence. Of course, these are also used in the programs themselves to maintain audience interest and to make sure people "stay tuned [to the same channel]."

The challenge for the visual media is that it is difficult to maintain high quality programming continuously. This became especially challenging once television programs began airing around the clock, including news, sports, and weather channels. While some channels have succeeded in doing so, many others fill our screens with vapid material. One cannot spend several hours watching some television or Internet programs without feeling empty or unpleasantly stimulated. The wasted feeling multiplies from a plethora of commercials (now abundant also on the Internet), even when they are clever or entertaining in themselves. Paying to eliminate commercials through various subscription or streaming services does not necessarily guarantee better content overall.

Nevertheless, many of us stay glued to our video screens much of the time. Older generations, having grown up with television, feel most comfortable with it. Younger generations seem to prefer videos they can access with their laptops or smartphones. In the coming-of-age of television in the 1950s and 60s, there was great concern that people, especially youth, were spending all their free time sitting and watching the screen. That worry has continued in the digital age, with new screens to engage with on laptops and smartphones in addition to television. The problem may even be worse because of the mobility of many digital platforms: people can stay connected to their screens anywhere they go, not just in their homes as with television. Indeed, on the sidewalks and even the roads, one sees many people looking down at their toys, not ahead where they are going (including some who are driving cars). Some of what they watch may be more static content like text messages or social posts, but the dynamic of a screen that can bring fresh fare frequently captures the attention even so.

Video screens may have put us in thrall over the past century, but they have also brought countless benefits that should be acknowledged as well. Through their content video screens have vastly expanded our horizons geographically, artistically, and recreationally. For all its insipid programming, television has some outstanding programs of a recurring or special kind. Whether these are special sports events like the Olympics and World Series, nature programs featuring exotic animals and habitats, theatrical or drama series, concerts classical or rock, talk shows, news programs... nowadays one has literally hundreds of channels from which to choose to find quality programs that can expand one's knowledge and horizons or provide good entertainment. The visual information conveyed by video screens can bring unparalleled awareness of many places, people, and things one would otherwise not know about. Even for a voracious reader of newspapers, books, and magazines, the best content on screen can be a primary resource and rich supplement.

Great artists of the modern era have exploited the video medium to our lasting benefit. These include actors, directors, screenwriters, cinematographers, and all others who put together a production for the screen. Cinema was the first platform for such creativity in the first half of the twentieth century, and it continues to capture large audiences with some first-rate issues. The popularity of movie stars and, to a lesser extent, directors demonstrates its influence. From Humphrey Bogart to Meryl Streep, Katharine Hepburn to Leonardo DiCaprio, Orson Welles and Ingmar Bergman to George Lucas and Steven Spielberg, the string of first-rate actors and directors in cinema (not to mention the support people behind them) has enriched our culture tremendously.

Television likewise has provided a forum for top-notch talent. Because of the numerous programs that are run-of-the-mill entertainment, this may not always be apparent. But others clearly involve the best writers, directors, and television actors or personalities available. That is why my sister, a medievalist, once said that if he were alive today, Geoffrey Chaucer (of *Canterbury Tales* fame) would be involved in television. I imagine he might be doing documentaries like Ken Burns or exposés like Michael Moore.

Our video screens have also become educational forums. Television features popular do-it-yourself home improvement programs, and Internet videos explain how to fix or operate a myriad of different things. Online courses present lectures and demonstrations, some of them part of a specific degree program and others open to all who are interested (so-called MOOCs). Video screens have not substantially replaced classroom teaching, but they offer helpful supplements even where the latter is the primary vehicle.

More recently, video has become a major form of communication, both personal and professional. For years the teleconference (via telephone) was the chief means of long-distance communication, and one can even remember how difficult it was to connect more than two people before group conference lines became freely available. Then video conferencing became the new thing, but only in offices with the expensive equipment to enable it. Finally, with Internet programs like Skype or Zoom, a number of people can now connect on their computers visually as well as aurally at little or no charge. This is a real boon, as it makes the communication much more immediate and complete. Parents with children away from home especially appreciate seeing them on the screen.

No doubt as technology advances there will be more innovative ways video screens can improve our lives. Because of their capability to grab and hold our attention, however, video screens will always be a mixed blessing whose application has to be monitored carefully against overuse or misuse. The visual medium can certainly be used as a form of escapism, since television and movies can provide nearly constant diversion from other aspects of our lives. In this respect video screens are a greater temptation than more traditional forms of entertainment like reading books and attending theater, which require more effort on the part of the recipient and have distinct beginnings and endings. Video in its most extreme form – so-called virtual reality – can even replace the real world around us with a simulated one. While this can be useful for entertainment and training purposes, its extension more generally, as suggested by some high-tech people, would divorce people even more from the world in which they live.

Video screens can enrich our lives and fulfill many human needs, but they should never become an alternative reality on a permanent basis.

Death and Predation

WHAT IS IT ABOUT our world that it must be based on death and predation? Are other kinds of worlds possible without them, and what might they look like?

Ours is a richly renewed world because of birth, and a sadly limited one because of death. For the individual, aging diminishes and death terminates all that a person is and can be. For society, there are cares and expenses from the dying process, but the emphasis on youth and change (in most Western societies) ensures that the focus is on birth. Society does not generally mourn the passing of individuals, treating it as factual news, but instead rewards movement forward from the young.

Now, the existence of birth and death does not necessarily mean that society changes and develops, as many societies have stayed constant through the generations. It is more likely, though, that change will occur when new individuals with their genetic variation emerge over time. The birth process in all but an ingrown society provides this potential. Without the culling of individuals by death on the other end, however, society could be paralyzed and the weight of the past could persist unproductively. Potentially serious conflicts could result between young and old – more than we currently experience, with the aged eventually bowing out.

Death is an essential part of nature on Earth. A big part of any ecosystem is devoted to the recycling of nutrients and biological matter from dead plants and animals, and without the small and large organisms that perform this function, life would not be able to continue in most places. As in human society, change is enabled through the process of death and birth and genetic variation (often in response to environmental changes). Through such change and the mechanism of natural selection, species and ecosystems adapt to the world and develop new ways of coping with it in what we call evolution.

Enter predation as a particularly focused and ruthless form of death. Ecology teaches how important predator-prey relationships are and how they foster healthier species and ecosystems. The ecologist views the dynamic as essential to evolution, since it culls the weaker, less adapted members of a species. It also keeps various species in balance, ensuring that prey do not overpopulate their habitat (as with deer in the absence of their predators) and that predators remain at a level supported by their prey. If one accepts that animals can functionally eat other animals, predation seems to be a likely outcome. Not all species need be gatherers or scavengers,[10] while husbandry is practiced only by a few species (humans, ants) and just makes the predation more domesticated.

In this system nature seems to place more value on the species or group than on the individual.[11] For humans growing up in cultures that value the individual, this can be a callous result. We have all seen nature films of predatory interaction (I cannot watch these dispassionately, however I try), and nature lovers and hikers have seen it happen live or seen the results or remains. Don't believe the myth that the act of predation is swift and prey barely know what hits them. I don't demonize predators; I just feel sorry for their prey. It does, after all, seem uncivil to eat someone else: the life of another being is used to maintain one's own, which is thereby valued more highly. This may be appropriate for the Triassic, Jurassic, and Cretaceous periods, with their ungainly and terrifying creatures (the dinosaurs), but not for our supposedly gentler one. Except there are so many species today that do just that, including, of course, our own.

A world without death and predation would be very different indeed. A world based just on birth without death would not last very long.

---

[10] One can conjecture that predation began when some organism chose to eat another's lunch by eating the other organism whole. Of course, predation in some form appears to occur at all levels, including cellular, and may truly be endemic to our form of life.

[11] See also "Nature's Cruelty."

Species upon species would over-populate their habitats, and resources would become scarce and eventually non-existent. There would, in essence, be a protoplasm spasm on Earth that would make life unlivable. What would result is conjecture, since the premise is that death does not happen.

In a more fanciful world, which we may postulate as having neither birth nor death, there would be a timeless state of being enjoyed by a limited set of (immortal) individuals. The Greeks and Romans in part invented this in their concept of the gods (who also had special powers). But it raises many questions, such as when the aging process starts and stops, whether individual development occurs forever or is frozen in an eternal sameness, or whether circumstances similarly can change.

As for predation, ecologists have conjectured what a world of vegetarians would look like, with the reduced energy flow involved (think cows grazing and not moving too fast). I would prefer such a world where species would not kill others, but the type of species that could evolve therefrom might be seriously limited. Arguably, the entire tree of evolution would look different if predation were not a key factor in species survival, either as predators or prey. It may be difficult to accept that species would not learn very much if they didn't have to hunt or avoid being eaten. Would they have emerged from the sea, or taken to the air? Would far fewer species have evolved, mainly by genetic mutation? And would life have even survived on Earth with much slower and limited adaptations as these?

Until we can grow meat on trees (and provide it to all other carnivores), we seem locked in a world of predation. In fact, most humans are not vegetarian and, as omnivores, would physically have difficulty being one. Other carnivorous species have evolved this way and instinctively go for the jugular. I empathize with human vegetarians but feel that such abstention makes little difference in this world of predator and prey.

Yet, we may wonder about the potentially negative implications of death by predation for humans. Does the ubiquity of this kind of killing make other, less acceptable kinds of killing more likely? After all, criminals prey on the weak, the old, and the infirm, like all predators; while theirs is a form of cannibalistic predation (on their own species), they are following a well-established pattern in nature (even the cannibalistic part). Human society does not tolerate this application of natural law to itself, but the model is irresistible to the ruthless.

On a more philosophical level, what does predation as well as death tell us about whatever is behind the creation of the universe and our place in it? Certainly, a system dependent on so much killing and pain can not be the work of a humane creator. If death from disease, age, or accident is so difficult to reconcile with a loving deity (and Western religions spend much time trying to do so), how much more disturbing is death at the paw or jaw (or DNA) of another.

The premise of a humane or loving creator behind it all may be in question, but that leaves us with the human tendency toward morality and humaneness, and how these evolved in this jungle. While I believe these are largely human constructs,[12] I think we should cherish, nurture, and apply them through all our dealings. Though they may run counter to some natural forces and our own instincts, they ultimately make us better humans and make our lives – and those of all we affect – more fulfilling and positive. This does not require that we be vegetarian, but that we use other animals in the most humane way possible.

We might envy a state of eternal sameness, free of death and predation, living like the gods of ancient mythology. But on closer inspection our world of birth and death appears to be more viable and interesting, however sad, tragic, or painful the death and predatory process may be. But I still don't like that part of it.

---

[12] The loving impulse behind morality and humaneness is, nevertheless, shared by some other species, as discussed in the final essay.

Love and Disaffection

WHAT IS IT ABOUT romantic love that it can so easily turn negative and even vitriolic? And how does this compare with other kinds of love and with friendship?

Rare is the couple whose first romantic love became the only one. For most all of us, it takes several tries to find the "right" person. All the other relationships start off well but do not work out well. Sometimes this happens amicably, sometimes tumultuously, but always with a final balance of negative feelings about a relationship that was once so positive.

As in any human relationship, two people in romantic love get to know each other better over time. The greater intimacy of romantic love may accelerate this process, or else the focus on romance may distract from aspects of the relationship that work less well. It is natural, though, that as people learn more about each other they will either feel more positively or begin to have doubts about the relationship. When the latter happens in a romantic relationship, it can proceed quickly as the good feelings become displaced by bad ones. The very intimacy that previously forged the relationship can make these adverse feelings more intensely felt and repugnant to the one who has them.

Romantic love gains its strength from both mind and body. It involves not only our feelings but also the hormones that keep our species going. It is thus a very strong and deeply based emotion, arguably a biologically driven impulse to which all are susceptible. It is most certainly a fire within us, and anything that upsets it can inflame it. That is why the tender feelings of romance can easily transmogrify into anger and recrimination. Moreover, both romantic love and its inverse feed off passion and are susceptible to uncontrolled eruptions.

But something more is involved in romantic love to cause it later to flip to anger and bitterness. Why wouldn't the positive passion involved just move on elsewhere once the relationship sours?

Certainly, there is a real letdown, and sadness and even depression may result from the now-unfulfilled love. But people do often deal with the change calmly and reasonably, even remaining friends.

In many cases, however, the former lover is now seen as a bad person, full of faults and deficiencies. Traits initially viewed as charming or excusable precipitate outrage in the other and are blamed for the breakup. The high expectations the lovers held for the relationship and the trust they innately felt toward one another disintegrate into disillusion and suspicion. Worse, one or both of the lovers may feel betrayed – that the other person is not who he or she presented themselves to be, or else promises made in the throes of early love are not kept. This sense of betrayal, combined with and fueled by passion, can lead to very negative behavior.

The way romantic love evolves from the beginning to its later phases can also cause a precipitous change in feelings. Everything can seem right at the start of a relationship, which we speak of colloquially as the honeymoon phase, as nature takes care to distort our perception for the promotion of a union. We say someone "falls" in love and is "smitten" about another. Friends may even wonder what the besotted sees in the loved one. The wise adage about looking carefully before committing to a relationship and being more tolerant afterward is frequently ignored and observed in the reverse. Lovers tend to rationalize away any concerns about a relationship at the beginning and become overly critical later when they are even more involved in it.

The unrealistically positive beginning to romantic love can have a deleterious effect later, when blemishes in the relationship or the other person become undeniable. It can make the contrast between the two images of the relationship greater and consequently the promise of it more broken. This may happen even if the beloved does not pretend to be as good as he or she was perceived to be.

High passions and expectations characterize romantic love and distinguish it from other forms of love and friendship. So-called platonic love is by definition dispassionate, rooted predominantly in mind rather than body. Such love is based more on admiration than on desire or need, and so the platonic lover does not expect to receive anything in return. Disappointment may still result if the loved one falls short by some objective measure, but it will not be accompanied by a sense of betrayal. In the still rarer case of romantic but selfless love, the lover is motivated more by concern for the loved one than by what the lover may receive in return. In this case any personal disappointment is mitigated by acceptance and cheerful fulfillment of the loved one's wishes.

Friendship is characterized by less of all of these – passion, expectations, needs, and trust. All may figure to some extent in friendship, but at a much lower level than with romantic love. Perhaps the strongest such feeling is trust, followed by need. People expect their friends to keep their word, not speak ill of them to others, and not act against their own interests. Betrayal of this trust can cause anger, and friends can become bitter toward each other. But the level of such emotion is usually less than with lovers. Of course, the closer a friendship tends toward love – and there is always an element of love in friendship – the more likely the reaction will be as with lovers. This depends also on the extent to which friendship is based on need. Again, typically lovers need each other more than friends do, but paradoxically the relationships of friends generally last longer, perhaps as a result.

In our current culture where about half of all marriages end in divorce, romantic love may seem a risky route to a permanent relationship. Getting to marriage typically involves a much greater number of failed relationships. Knowing that romantic affairs often evolve from ecstasy to negativity, we may wonder whether a more deliberate approach is warranted. Is there really a benefit in – to paraphrase Samuel Johnson – the triumph of hope and hormones over experience?

To doubters of romantic love I counter in two ways. First, our biological nature will not permit us to suppress or eliminate romantic love. It is truly built into our genes as a way to maintain the human species. The attraction that two people feel toward each other is often lathered in love precisely to effectuate a union that might otherwise be thwarted by more objective perception. Writers, artists, and composers have glorified the emotion of love; they have also faithfully probed its less pleasant and even tragic side. But nothing has diminished the power of romantic love in individuals.

Beyond the biological imperatives of romantic love, it can truly be one of the most rewarding and wonderful experiences of life. Romantic love feels so good at the beginning because it really is so good. The alternative of a purely sexual interaction between people or a completely "deliberate," objective selection of mate (as in prearranged marriage) saps a relationship of its vitality, spontaneity, and joy. Giving love can be the greatest gift one can bestow, while being loved is deliciously validating. That human love also comes with strings of attachment like needs and expectations does not vitiate its giving side. Any human relationship can go bad, and the fact that so many romantic ones do can be ascribed to the elevated stakes involved. But not to engage in this arena is to miss an entire dimension of life. The triumph of hope over experience is just that.

Polarized

WHAT IS IT ABOUT human views that they tend so much to the extremes of an issue? Why can't people see both sides, and what does taking one side or the other satisfy that the middle ground does not?

Certainly in politics, people who have strong beliefs about a topic belong to one side or the other and rarely represent the middle ground. The very existence of political parties, which strive to differentiate themselves from the others, demonstrates the polarization. During some periods the parties may, in fact, find common ground between them; but even then, there are usually aspects of an issue on which they do not agree. More typically, political parties stake out diametrically opposed viewpoints that their members and supporters rally behind vehemently. Efforts at subsequent compromise or "bipartisanship" are left to professional politicians and legislators. Sometimes, as in the current U.S. political climate, attempts by the professionals to reach across the divide may actually be viewed as heresy by party activists.

What is lacking is not only organized support in the middle but enthusiasm for centrist positions. Rarely do we see a passionate centrist; moderation colors the emotion as well as the position taken. In fact, many in the middle of an issue tend to be apathetic, caring not much one way or the other. They might see the merits of both positions but not care enough about them; or, they aren't convinced that either of the more extreme positions is entirely correct, and they fall back on the in-between as neutral or safe ground. In any case, they probably won't be demonstrating for the middle position or arguing with others on its behalf.

The problem is that few people actually forge a coherent middle position that can be supported enthusiastically. Seeing the merits of both sides is a good start and something that everyone should do (but generally do not). Merely to appreciate both sides, however, results in an ambivalent or eclectic position or none at all. It takes real thought to see how the needs of both sides may be accommodated, something like the process of mediation. Even better is to fashion a solution to the problem that subsumes the two extremes through an entirely different approach.

A classic case of the latter in conservation politics is to protect a valuable ecosystem that also has economic resource value by giving the local people jobs related to tourism, sustainable harvesting, and stewardship of the land. By not consuming the resource, it can continue to generate economic benefit indefinitely. The more conventional, mediated solution might be to divide the land into protected and exploited areas. Neither of these solutions satisfies the two more extreme positions of either complete exploitation or complete preservation, but the more creative one comes close.

Fashioning a middle ground, especially a creative solution, takes more effort than devising extreme positions. The extremes often take a more simplistic view of the problem and its potential resolution, conveniently leaving out facts that don't fit the viewpoint. The vehemence of supporters of either extreme of an issue may, indeed, be indicative of their imperfect solutions to it. But a creative, well-constructed solution in the middle may be more complex to explain. It may not satisfy today's need for instant messages, catchy phrases, and winning elevator speeches. This makes it difficult to inspire the enthusiasm and vigor partisans on either side can marshal.

Moreover, taking a centrist position that requires understanding both sides can create cognitive dissonance that adds discomfort to complexity. When arguing a position one doesn't want to concede to the other side that it has valid points. A middle view, by definition, incorporates reasonable concerns on either side, but they are often in apparent conflict that can be resolved only with more integrative thinking. This requires considering simultaneously two ostensibly incompatible positions, and most of us aren't equipped to do so easily. This explains not only the challenge of thinking in the middle, but also the allure of taking more extreme positions that exclude the other side.

Human views on significant issues thus tend to extreme positions because they are easier to formulate, understand, explain, argue, and justify. But there is more – a deeper need that is satisfied by taking sides in a partisan way. The deeper need has both sociological and psychological components.

Most partisans relish the sense of belonging to a group of like-minded people, who make them feel more comfortable and secure. In addition, partisans are reinforced in their views by discussing them with others in their group. They can nod knowingly and confidently when a position is stated, believing sincerely that no other viewpoint could possibly be right because they are hearing no other. Political parties are prime examples of this sociology of viewpoints, and their quadrennial conventions are blatant demonstrations of the uniformity it generally fosters, with myriad waving signs saying the same thing. (Occasionally, a divisive issue causes things to get ugly, like internecine warfare, but this is strenuously avoided by party leaders.) In essence, banding together according to viewpoint is a form of tribalism, as it strengthens support for a position through sheer numbers and opposes other views in an organized way.

The psychological need satisfied by partisan positions mirrors in reverse the apathy of the middle. If centrists prefer not getting worked up by issues, partisans relish doing just that. One can legitimately feel strongly about many political and social issues, since they relate to people's welfare, economic viability, and security in the world. But the unwillingness to consider other viewpoints fuels a passion and rancor that many partisans gleefully embrace and seek to stoke in others. This puts partisanship on a different level that takes on the character of a game, even a sport (many have likened politics to a sport, for example), with the rallying, the binary identities, the episodes of winning and losing. In short, being partisan is a ticket to an exciting experience, one that might just overcome the tedium of life.

In summary, people tend to take either side of an issue rather than the middle because it is easier and because doing so joins them with like-minded individuals as well as adds zest to their lives. Partisans eschew the middle for the simplicity and rewards of the extremes.

Taking Dictation

WHAT IS IT ABOUT the people who support dictators that they are so willing to prop up an evil, narcissistic man? What do they gain from him, and how does their relationship differ from support for more democratic candidates?

The dictators considered here broach no dissent in their countries or abroad, dispatch their political foes ruthlessly, and maintain popular support through repeated lies and fear-mongering. Contemporary examples include Vladimir Putin of Russia, Kim Jong Un of North Korea, and Rodrigo Duterte of the Philippines. Close behind, but more subtle in his use of power, is Xi Jinping of the (so-called) People's Republic of China. There are also would-be dictators in other countries, some close to home.

To the extent a country is ruled absolutely, it is difficult to determine who actually supports a dictator as distinct from acquiescing in a situation beyond one's control. There are those who directly help the dictator gain power in an authoritarian way, and those among the population at large who support this move. Our concern is primarily with the latter, as the former typically benefit directly from their association with the dictator in terms of derivative power or wealth.

As background I refer the reader to another essay, "Evil," which offers several possible explanations for our fascination with evil, of which two seem germane here. People to some extent identify with a bad guy as an alter ego who makes them feel strong and expresses forbidden desires and acts. This allows them not to acknowledge or play out their own evil. Also, aligning with the bad guy provides vicarious indulgence in the illicit pleasures and benefits he enjoys.

Supporters of dictators among the people do, indeed, seem to gravitate to a "strongman" (word used advisedly, as there are scarcely any historical female dictators). The attraction he garners goes beyond support for the hot-button issues he exploits, although these are used effectively to whip up emotions and false enemies. Certainly, the strongman convinces his supporters that he looks after their interests where others have not and that he alone will make them safe and prosperous. But beyond these promised benefits, the strongman provides people a psychological crutch in their lives, an external source of strength they lack of their own. They feel empowered by his bold talk and action. They feel entitled because of him to express their grievances and prejudices. His success in rising to the top justifies feelings and actions they have suppressed because they are otherwise socially unacceptable. And so the dictator gives these people vicarious strength and the license to be mean. That their actual status in life does not change is compensated by these other presumed benefits they receive.

The strongman dynamic differs significantly from the relationship between a more democratic public figure and his or her supporters. A dictator employs fear and prejudice to galvanize support by heightening people's insecurity and providing a target for their unease. By demonizing a bogeyman enemy, a dictator creates a false problem and offers a phony solution to people's real problems. The narcissistic leader accrues affection the same way a bully does – through aggrandizement of self and vicarious gratification in others. A more democratic leader focuses on real issues and what might actually benefit the people. Prejudices and fears are not exploited (witness President Franklin Roosevelt's famous line about fighting fear itself), and others are not made to be the enemy falsely. While some democratic leaders do stir up people's emotions both about the issues and about themselves, the focus is on the cause they represent rather than aggrandizement of the leader.

Dictators also differ from democratic leaders by taking extreme positions on issues and asking for mindless acceptance of these views from their followers. Extremism fits the autocrat's personality, which tends toward hyperbole, dogmatism, and emotionalism. Using these distorted and oversimplified approaches to issues, the dictator creates an unwarranted sense of urgency if not desperation in his followers. Furthermore, only through drastic actions by the dictator – often illegal and destructive of the social fabric – can the alleged danger be abated.

Democratic leaders do not tend to peddle in extremist views. Whether they are on the "left" or "right" of the spectrum, they recognize the basic norms of a democratic society and the need to adhere to facts and ethical behavior. Distortions do occur in political discourse and campaigns, and all parties are guilty at times of unjustifiably maligning their opponents. But democratic leaders we admire are known primarily for the positive visions they offer the people. President John F. Kennedy inspired an entire younger generation to public service to address social problems in the United States and abroad, and he thrilled most of the country by his vision of a "new frontier" of space exploration, global leadership, and national commitment. Similarly, the late Senator John McCain worked tirelessly against totalitarian regimes around the world, and he maintained a vision of the United States as a beacon of freedom and human rights to all people that made him admired around the world.

Supporters of such democratic leaders may well get caught up in the rhetoric of the leaders and become enthusiastic and emotional about the visions they espouse. But they don't proceed to denigrate other citizens, other races, or other religions as a result. And that is the real distinction between followers of democratic leaders and followers of dictators. The latter accept a distorted, untruthful version of reality painted by the dictator, and they embrace it mindlessly and irrationally. They willingly buy into the venomous lies and hatreds spewed out by the dictator. Ultimately, this mob-like support gives the dictator license to commit heinous acts against his alleged enemies *within* the country he rules. Political opponents, minorities, outspoken critics, and the media may be targeted and exterminated. This may lead to the "societal evil" described in the aforementioned essay, where nearly everyone becomes implicated by their tacit compliance with the autocrat's lies and deeds.

There will always be evil, narcissistic men in public life, but they would go nowhere were it not for the people in their inner circle and at large who support them. The former are no less evil than the dictator and differ only in being less charismatic and effective at garnering power. It is the people at large who have the ultimate responsibility to thwart dictatorship. Some of a dictator's supporters may genuinely suffer from economic and social deprivation and seek desperately for help. But even they cannot ignore the basis on which the purported assistance is being offered. The rest of the supporters either revel in the dictator's lies and prejudices or rationalize them on behalf of some other supposed good he will deliver. None of these responses is acceptable in a civilized society.

Optimistic Fatalism

WHAT IS IT ABOUT when people express optimism when bad things happen? Do they really believe it, and what does it signify?

I refer to a type of expression commonly heard these days in response to unfortunate events. It takes various forms, including: "it's for the best," "it was meant to be," "things happen for a reason," or, more strangely, "the universe wants/doesn't want that." Young men often hear the first phrase from girlfriends breaking up with them. Mothers are also fond of the phrase to calm family in emotionally troubled times. The last phrase has sprung up in recent years from unknown sources, perhaps astrological.

The attitude or belief behind these expressions is not necessarily religious, although it is consistent with religious beliefs and may be informed by them. Religious people often believe that important events in life are guided divinely, since God in Western religions is omnipotent and can potentially control everything in life (with some "free will" allowed for humans to be tested). But the belief considered here is non-denominational and even secular, espoused by many who are not at all religious.

The belief maintains with considerable confidence that however bad things may be now, there is some force out there ensuring they will turn out better in the future. Moreover, the current situation is a necessary precondition for things to improve. I call this optimistic fatalism because it paradoxically shares characteristics that historically have been opposite. One does not think of fatalism as a very optimistic outlook, since fate is not necessarily favorably disposed to humans. "Fateful" is an allied word that similarly expresses foreboding, while "fatal," from the same root, now actually connotes death or demise. Optimistic fatalism, on the other hand, holds that everything always works out for the best even when specific events do not appear to.

This belief is the ultimate comfort thought in a life full of vicissitudes. It is popular because it completely solves a key problem of life: whatever happens, including misfortunes, can be considered at least partly positive, since it will be counterbalanced ultimately by good results. Someone's death will (it is believed) become the catalyst for a movement that overcomes the cause of it; a painful breakup between two people will (it is believed) lead to a better life for each; a bad accident for a child will (it is believed) cause him to be more careful in the future and avoid worse injury; and so on. The strength of the belief may remain undiminished even when future events do not improve in the expectation that things will eventually turn out for the better. Since the future is open, that turn may always be just around the corner.

There has probably always been a sense of fatalism about life, since so much of it is out of any individual's control. The country, family, and historical period into which one is born; the political, economic, and social events that occur in one's life; the actions of others; the health or sickness one endures; and "acts of God" are among the many events over which one has little or no control but which are nevertheless influential in one's life. One indeed swims in the current of life, affecting one's own course but in most cases being carried along more strongly than one can entirely control. It is understandable that one might believe that events are, if not preordained, beyond one's complete control.

Common expressions underscore this sense of fatalism. The popular saying, "Que sera, sera" (whatever will be, will be), and the contemporary one, "It is what it is," both acknowledge that control of events, present and future, is mostly external to the speaker. Note, however, that the underlying attitude of these expressions is at best neutral, if not slightly pessimistic. In contrast, optimistic fatalism takes the implied fatalism of these two and adds an important optimistic twist. Versions consistent with this view would be, "Que sera, eventualmente sera mejor" (whatever will be, will eventually be better), and, "It is what it is, but overall things will become better."

It is reasonable to ask whether optimistic fatalists actually believe in their viewpoint. It is one thing to hope that good will come out of misfortune and that bad events will turn out well in the end, or to try to see in every occurrence, however dire, a "silver lining." Also to be differentiated is an attitude of "making the best" out of everything; this helpful approach requires no postulate about the future but rather tries to extract whatever good can be derived from every situation. Optimistic fatalism goes beyond hope or positive attitude to assert that a better outcome will in fact transpire. Its adherents want to believe this, and some hold fast to it for security. Whether the belief could withstand truly harsh conditions and outcomes is uncertain. Mostly, it is the parlance of people who are not terribly unfortunate.

In any case, there is nothing inherently wrong with optimistic fatalism as a belief system, assuming it can be maintained. It is essentially the same as religious belief in a deity whose workings may be mysterious but are always just, so-called divine providence. The only danger of the belief, aside from potential disappointment and disillusionment, is that it may preclude trying to improve or prevent bad situations oneself. Faced with difficulty, one should look carefully at the situation and what led to it in an effort to avoid similar difficulties in the future and to resolve the current one. A fatalistic attitude can rob someone of the motivation to do these things.

My own view is less wishful than optimistic fatalism but just as hopeful. I am equally an optimist in believing that things *can* be better, that humans have the capability to improve themselves and the world they steward. I have hope but not belief that all will turn out well. My acquaintances who are optimistic fatalists often misconstrue this as pessimism and may even get peevish when I see darkness ahead. But I am realistic about the future, while idealistically wanting it to be better. We should work toward what is right and good and do our best despite what we cannot control ("fate"). Complacently expecting that good will always result may be understandable as a balm for present problems, but it is not an inducement to overcome them.

Written Words

WHAT IS IT ABOUT writing that makes it so much more difficult than speaking for most people? And why is writing virtually alone among the arts in being formally reviewed and modified by others before it is issued?

As I write here I confront a nearly blank page, with just the title and introduction above and some notes below to follow. The blank slate that invites creativity can also paralyze by its emptiness and lack of form. Even if we have something "to say" and would have no trouble speaking it, the empty page(s) demands more thought before we start writing. We generally have no trouble summoning our words and thoughts when we talk to others extemporaneously, but if asked to write these down we take greater care to express ourselves precisely and in an organized way. Perhaps because of its greater permanence, writing has a formality that demands more care from the start.

Our schooling focused on writing – literally, how to do so with our hands, then how to write grammatically and clearly – much more than on improving our speech. As much as this might have enhanced our writing abilities, arguably it more likely inhibited their natural flow. Who could forget the many paragraphs and essays we were forced to write and the myriad corrections and comments they inspired in our teachers? If comparable instruction were imposed on our speech, we might all be quite mute.

Another inhibiting factor in writing is that it is done through another medium. When we talk we simply voice words that our mind provides; when we write, we have to put these words on an external medium, whether pen on paper or computer keyboard on screen. No doubt such a medium provides advantages in making words more permanent than speech. The written word was a great advance for civilization, and it continues to be a fundamental aspect of life today. But it adds another mechanical level to expression that complicates its translation from the mind to outside. This effect may also vary depending on the particular medium on which we write. I know that my own writing can be subtly affected by whether it is done on paper, on a typewriter (in former days), or on a word-processing computer.

Speaking allows forms of expression less tolerated in writing, and it also provides non-verbal information absent in writing. Almost all forms of speaking today, including before an audience, allow for a level of informality that most writing does not. We can speak with words and phrases, even slang, that only a very casual form of writing would allow. The choice of words in speech tends to be looser and less precise because of the speed and flow, whereas writing is expected to have more proper diction. Listeners also tolerate speech that is less organized in its articulation of ideas, whereas readers grow impatient with disorganized writing (ironically, since they can go back and reread it). Moreover, someone speaking has additional cues to support what is being expressed – facial and bodily gestures, inflections in the speech, emphasis given to particular words, etc. – that are almost entirely lacking in writing. This subliminal communication enriches the meaning of spoken words and can compensate for less precision in their choice. Conversely, writing must rely solely on the written words to convey the author's intent.

Although writing may be more difficult than speaking, its very challenges can provide compensating benefits. Clearer organization of ideas, more careful choice of words, and better grammar and expression are among the advantages of writing, due to the extra time and care it requires. Not by accident do we say that we want to "think something through on paper" before we discuss it with someone. Moreover, we can review what we say in writing and improve it before it is published or released, whereas the spoken word cannot be withdrawn once aired. Of course, what is written can become a permanent public record as well. There is an aphorism in the governmental world of Washington, D.C., never to write down what you wouldn't want to see printed in the *Washington Post*.

Perhaps because of the very difficulties of writing as well as its permanence, written works are almost universally subject to review before formal issuance. No company or government agency would allow a written document to go public without layers of review. While the focus is obviously on policy and positioning rather than on grammar and style, the latter often figure into the edits such reviews involve. For style especially affects the image of an institution, and managers are particularly sensitive to meta-messages in public communications. One of the big transitions staff make in going into management is to incorporate this perspective in the writing they produce or review.

Journalists are routinely subject to editing. In fact, management in the journalistic field is designed around the concept, with "Editor" a ubiquitous position title. There are numerous editors at various levels in any major newspaper or magazine, and typically an Editor-in-Chief or Executive Editor runs the entire enterprise (along with the publisher, depending on the arrangement). Journalistic editing maintains proper grammar, a consistent style for the particular journal, and a check on editorial opinion. Good editors also improve the clarity and economy of the writing. While such editing is more critical in journals with short deadlines, such as daily newspapers, it is pervasive throughout the industry.

Even professional authors have their works edited by professional editors. I refer here not to professionals who happen to write books in their fields and who are not necessarily the best writers (although some may well be, such as the eminent late scientists Loren Eiseley and Steven Jay Gould). Rather, those authors who make a living by writing, whether fiction or non-fiction, still have editors at their publishing houses. They often have a particular editor who suits their style and with whom they have a long association in producing their works, often acknowledged explicitly by the authors. No doubt the most famous and popular authors have considerable say in any editorial changes, but not without some review and discussion with the house.

One wonders how far back professional authors have been reviewed by editors. Shakespeare has many editors in modern times, but their function has been to ferret through the various folio editions to find the most authentic ones and to explain what archaic expressions mean. It is doubtful that (whoever he actually was) Shakespeare worked through an editor at the publisher of his plays – nor likely Donne, Marvell, Pope, Johnson, Milton, Keats, etc. The process may have changed later in the nineteenth century, but certainly became commonplace since the twentieth, when all authors have worked through an editor. Again, the most famous authors probably have considerable say in what is finally produced. But this may not occur without an argument, as even William Faulkner in his celebrated work, *The Sound and the Fury*, had to wrestle with his editor on formats he wished to use for the complex narrative.

The formal review and editing of literature stand in stark contrast to art works in other forms, whether music composition, painting, plastic arts, theater, dance, etc. Some of these works necessarily emanate from the artist untouched by others – typically paintings, sculpture, and other plastic arts, which cannot easily be modified once created. Composers may seek review from a mentor or trusted source, but they do not generally have the work "edited" by the sponsor or publisher. In stage works such as plays, opera, and dance, there is more opportunity for and likelihood of external review resulting in modifications by the creator or others as a work is realized in rehearsal. This process, which can result in significant changes in a work, tends to be *ad hoc* rather than a formal "edit" the work must undergo to be performed.

Classical music provides good examples of the range of these interactions, none to my knowledge akin to the editing process for writing (except in conservatory instruction). Orchestral and chamber works of yesterday and today do not generally get edited before publication or performance, except voluntarily by the composer from solicited reviews or from problems exposed during rehearsal. Some conductors and composers have chosen to alter the works of others that have already been published, such as Stokowski's dramatic orchestrations of Bach pieces and Mahler's romanticized "strengthening" of Beethoven symphonies. Fortunately, the original works have always been maintained and these altered versions have fallen by the wayside.

Many classical works have, nevertheless, appeared in altered form as transcriptions, such as a piano reduction of a symphony or the use of another instrument or combination of instruments than in the original piece. Reductions are never meant to substitute for or change a musical work, but rather to put it in a more accessible form. Piano reductions are routinely used for rehearsals of pieces scored for orchestras when the full entourage is not needed. Furthermore, reductions have historically been a vital way for music to be disseminated before the advent of electronic reproduction. In the nineteenth century, when pianos became a common part of middle-class households, piano reductions brought many symphonies and operas directly into the home.

Transcribing pieces for different instruments has also been a common historical practice. Composers such as Bach and Vivaldi often took their own or other composers' works and transcribed them for a different combination of instruments. The intention was not usually to improve the original piece but rather to give it additional expression. A more modern example, the reverse of a reduction, occurred when Maurice Ravel took Mussorgsky's piano set, *Pictures at an Exhibition*, and scored it for full orchestra. Both versions are celebrated and played on the concert stage today.

Classical musical theater, specifically opera, has a somewhat different record of alteration, in keeping with its other theatrical counterparts. While there is usually no formal review and editing process, historical and modern operas are subject to some alteration in production. Often it is a matter of length and cost, where certain scenes may be eliminated from a production as superfluous. The composer may have written several versions of an aria or overture that can be selected by the music director (e.g., Beethoven's different "Leonora" overtures for *Fidelio*). Even Mozart's *Don Giovanni*, considered by many to be the greatest single opera, underwent numerous modifications from its initial performance. Right from the beginning, some lead singers demanded additional showcase arias or declined to sing others. In subsequent premiers in various European cities, versions with and without the final comedic sextet were performed (the opera otherwise ends with Don Juan consumed in flames as he goes to hell). Over the course of the nineteenth century, many additional alterations were made in various national productions of *Don Giovanni*, including rewrites of the many recitatives between arias or embellishments of some of the orchestration (e.g., adding more brass for greater effect). But overall, Mozart's score remained intact and the basis for performance. And today's productions are generally faithful to the original, with all the subsequent dross relegated to the historical wastebin where it belongs.

Most of these alterations in music occur after its initial composition and performance, in contrast to formal review of writing prior to publication. Perhaps the editing process of literature stems from its use in other forms of writing, such as journalism, as there isn't always a bright line between the two. Or, because writing expresses ideas and uses words that some may find offensive, blasphemous, or treasonous, publishing houses feel the need to protect themselves.

Until relatively recently, censorship of written material considered pornographic was common even in the free world.

Prose literature may lend itself more to editing because it is not usually considered as personal an art form. I suspect that editors of poetry and drama are less likely to make numerous edits of submitted works than editors of prose, although suggestions may be given as to certain passages, the tone or diction, the course of a narrative, a particular stretch of dialogue or scene, etc. All this is not to say that prose literature is in greater need of editing than other art forms or even speaking. Speaking can be difficult, too, in a more formal setting, such as in front of a large or important audience. In this case the "talk" is often reviewed and edited by others beforehand, just like a written document.

Those of us who write often in our work or write as a profession may well be fated to face the editor's scalpel. It can be devastating to see one's work slashed to pieces and rewritten in someone else's style. Worse yet may be a future edition "abridged" for simplification, as has sometimes been done with the classics. At some point the writer may rebel and throw off the editor's yoke through self-publishing, knowing that self-editing sometimes falls short in cleaning up one's prose. Or the writer may just put the editor in their proper place through such words as Faulkner wrote to his: "And don[']t make any more additions to the script, bud. I know you mean well, but so do I."[13]

---

[13] As quoted in Michael Millgate, "The Composition of *The Sound and the Fury*," from *The Achievement of William Faulkner* (London: Constable, 1965), pp. 86-103, 313-14.

My Two-Step

WHAT IS IT ABOUT my skills that despite their breadth and magnitude, the market never seems interested in employing them?

Take my special walking skill: when I am twenty to thirty feet away from a curb or sidewalk impediment, I sense infallibly which foot will land where and smoothly navigate the disturbance. Most people don't even look that far ahead, of course, so technically I could count that as another unrewarded skill. When they get to the blip in their walk, they have to take half steps or shift their feet to surmount or circumvent the obstacle. I, on the other hand, just keep walking ahead with nary a change in my gait.

This is a valuable skill, but the market doesn't seem to have a place for it. I've considered ways to adapt it to marketable activities like sports, marching bands, military parades, and modeling. In each case, there seem to be other requirements that, though of much lesser skill, capture the attention of talent scouts. For instance, they seem more interested in whether a person can throw a ball – or, more likely, stuff it – into an elevated hoop. Wouldn't it be better to see people on the court gauging their steps perfectly to reach the end lines and avoid stepping on lines in the middle, like baseball managers when they come out to change a pitcher? Likewise, models are hired for appearance only, and it doesn't seem to matter if the model comes to the end of a runway in a whole step or an awkward half-step before turning around. What a pity – with my talent they could be so much more graceful and avoid falling off the end – and the clothes would sell even better!

Then there's my ability to sense what time it is without having consulted a clock for hours. I can be within minutes of the exact time, sometimes right on it. I inquired long ago with businesses that need to run on time, like the television and radio networks, but they said they had timekeepers whose jobs are guaranteed under union rules. I also spoke with our national railroad, Amtrak, and they said my adherence to a schedule would put me in jeopardy of retaliation by other conductors and engineers. I finally gave up because most clocks and watches switched over to digital format, and my skill breaks down entirely with this display.

I can also go for hours without drinking water, even on a hot day or on a field outing or hike. I initially went to the water companies and water conservation districts to explain my skill, but the former shooed me away and the latter made me wait interminably in the foyer. Then, as my luck would have it, the bottled water companies started their campaign to make everyone think they will dry up if they don't carry water with them everywhere. I became a pariah to the marketplace, having a skill contrary to the best interests of the populace. Of course, over time it became apparent that the water thing was overblown and people were drinking water unnecessarily. But my skill might have carried the trend too far in the other direction, and the Madison Avenue types left me waiting in the foyer as well.

One skill I have just shocked me as to its unmarketability. I have an uncanny ability to perceive hypocrites even before they act or speak. I think I acquired this skill honestly, as my dad hated phonies, too. When a hypocritical person comes into my view, my nose turns up as in a stench and my face uncontrollably averts to one side or the other. I have had several embarrassing occasions where I had to control these reactions in greeting someone, but I steered clear of the person thereafter. While this skill might seem extraordinarily valuable in religion and politics, I was surprised how apprehensive people in those occupations became when I explained it to them. Even the two major political parties, to whom I offered my services, rebuffed me summarily; one practically threw me out of their headquarters, saying I was an existential threat.

The reader will be especially impressed by the next skill I possess. I discovered as a child that when I am about to sneeze, applying pressure with my index finger below my nose staves it off almost every time. This is such a valuable skill to have in a concert hall or funeral service, and it could be critical to survival in times of war and espionage. Yet, when I approached our army and intelligence agencies, they all thought I was making a secret sign for an undercover terrorist group, and I had to swear allegiance to leave their buildings. Now I have to suppress my sneezes in public furtively by maintaining a stiff upper lip all by itself.

Eventually I decided that my greatest asset was my own self. If these extraordinary skills were not valued in the marketplace individually, surely they would be in the aggregate. I had, after all, felt since my early childhood that I was an unusual person (why else did most other kids stay away from me?), so why couldn't that be the basis for my career? I searched in vain on occupation forms and career aptitude tests for "personhood," "unusual person," or "being him/herself." I was determined to blaze a new trail in the workaday world to allow for such a career, but I had no idea what it entailed or who would employ me.

Consequently, when it came to declaring a major in college, I chose the only one that didn't require me to forsake my special skills or learn new ones that might be useful in the marketplace: I became an English major. The occupation naturally emanating from this major with my special skills was to become a poet. I tried out for the college literary magazine, and they said my poems had potential. But the position they offered demanded that I run the business side of the rag as well. What a malevolent turn of events! My personhood was now to be used in the marketplace selling advertising space to local businesses. I politely declined.

There remained no alternative but to teach. Yet I continued to wonder, all these years since, just how many other people find their skills undervalued by society. Its priorities can be inexplicable. I know we need paramedics, doctors, police, and firemen, but lawyers and economists? sports stars and television celebrities? Over the long reach of civilized time, just think how many skills have gone unused, unfulfilled, unhelpful to society – even if they are not as special as mine. Imagine what they might have contributed, and how the world could have become a better place.

Fear of Death

WHAT IS IT ABOUT death that makes us so fear dying?

Nature normally inures us to the commonplace, but there is almost nothing we accept less than death. The reason may seem obvious: death is the antithesis to the survival instinct that is imbued in every living creature, what we are all programmed to avoid at almost all cost. If we did not fear it, we would be less likely to avoid it. Fear drives our fight-or-flight response to immediate (potentially mortal) danger. The risk of more gradual death, such as from disease, prompts us to avoid situations and conditions that may lead to it, with fear rising the closer we are to experiencing these. In short, fear of death is a key evolutionary mechanism to keep external dangers at bay long enough for creatures to reproduce and the species to survive.

Apart from this mostly instinctual response to death, we nevertheless maintain a fearful response even in reflecting on death in the abstract future. Generally, none of us knows when we will die; but virtually all of us shun the thought of our dying. We may make appropriate plans for the eventuality, such as by drawing up wills and estate plans. These may actually give a certain comfort – that life will continue through our families and possessions, that death is really a mundane matter – as we avoid the naked, solitary reality of death itself and what it means for *us*. It is in those quiet moments alone that the fear resumes. What will happen to my *self*? What does it mean for me to be non-existent, for my consciousness not only to be out of my control as in sleep, but completely out of commission for ever more? What unknowns might lurk in the deathly state? Is it the same as before we were born?

Along with our instinct for survival comes a strong instinct to align with and protect our sense of self. This is completely at risk in death, which appears to destroy it. Those with religious or spiritual beliefs in an afterlife following life on Earth may have this solved. But for the rest of us, the unknown nature of the deathly state and its apparent decimation of our very being – mind, body, and spirit –

strike at the heart of what we are. Nor can I believe that a spirit-like essence of ourselves survives after death. One can admire the "spirit" of many creatures, including humans, in terms of their energy and uniqueness as individuals. But it is a further step to believe that we are endowed with a spirit that survives the material disintegration of our bodies and minds in death. Looking at decaying plants and animals, it is to wonder how something else survives, and why. I also cannot imagine our world replete with billions of spirits from all creatures past and present (assuming humans are not the only ones so endowed).

Fear of death is not just a form of anxiety about one's life from feeling a lack of fulfillment and worry about time running out. Many very successful people have displayed notable fear of death (for example, the composers Mahler and Wagner), so if this is a factor it must reflect some deeper level of dissatisfaction. Nor is knowledge of the workings of death an antidote. Doctors, many of whom experience the causes of death daily, nonetheless face it like the rest of us, fearfully. And while older people may think about death much more because of its relative imminence, young people have no less a fear when they actually confront it, as when a friend dies. They just have the luxury of a time cushion and actuarial facts to put the unpleasantness far off in the future.

Of course, fear of death is not necessarily the dominant motivator in our lives at all times. Altruism, heroism, devotion to a cause, protection of family, etc. may overtake the fear and cause us to sacrifice ourselves. In this regard, it would be interesting to know if cultures that put less emphasis on the individual than the West experience less concern about dying. For if the fear of death is primarily motivated by loss of self, immersion of the latter in a larger entity (societal, sect, or clan) would potentially mitigate the fear. We must also consider to what degree social and economic factors might come into play, and whether those who live in much less comfortable and promising conditions have less concern about leaving it. Often this feeling is leavened by religious belief in a better afterlife, but it may also just be a sense of relief to leave this vale of tears.

Over the millennia and to this day, human culture has dealt with the fear of death in a variety of ways. While this would make a fascinating monograph in itself, a few examples here may help to illuminate the question we began with. Egyptian mummification attempted to preserve the deceased in a nearly intact state, and many of the person's possessions were kept in the vicinity to maintain a semblance of the life they had lived. Thus did they attempt to preserve the royal or important individual as such, minimizing the difference between life and death. In more recent Western culture a common device has been to personify death, as in Donne's poem, "Death, be not proud," or Bergman's classic movie, *The Seventh Seal.* This seems to make death less frightening, even if its corpus is skeletal or hollow, because it is at human scale, contained, and in some way known. Donne triumphs over death as a person by taunting it (we reap similar pleasures in sleep), castigating it (it is associated with poison, sickness, and bad people), and, ultimately, dismissing it (right after death comes eternal life), using religious salvation as the coup de grace. One cannot help but think that even Donne felt some fear, however, given the vehemence he puts into these assertions to counter what "some" have called "Mighty and dreadfull."

Other efforts to mitigate the fear of death are also telling. We are taught at an early age (as soon as death becomes permissible to discuss) that it is a "natural" part of life, just the ending. As some die, others are born, and the cycle renews. This works on a rational basis, but it falls short when someone realizes that he or she is the one who will eventually end and be replaced by a newborn. The approach attempts, not very successfully, to make belonging to a group – the society or species at large – sufficient compensation to overcome the loss of individual identity and being. Another rationale is that life could not continue to exist if nothing died, as biological systems depend on the constant renewal of death and birth. Again, this ecological view, while accurate, works on an intellectual basis but leaves us hanging emotionally, since our lives are based on our individual experiences and relationships, not on a Gaia-like consciousness of the entire world.

We may wonder how other animals deal with death. We have good evidence that certain social animals like elephants not only understand the loss of one of the herd but mourn for it as well. Parrots are notorious for grieving the loss of their companion human (as I have, in reverse). We also know that many animals sequester themselves at the end, going off the reservation to die in seclusion. What they know or sense about their ultimate end is a mystery to us anthropocentric beings. To what extent any species other than humans contemplates death as a future possibility, rather than a present danger, we also do not know.

One near-certain cure for humans not to fear death is to become carefree about life. We introverts often secretly envy extroverts (while openly criticizing them) for their apparent indifference to so many things that gnaw at us. But here the extroverts may have it solved: what will be, will be; it is as it is (a more stunning tautology I cannot imagine); go with the flow; etc. In other words, don't worry, take life as it comes. This may not guarantee a lack of fear at the end, but it may come closest to achieving that in the meantime.

Aside from religious beliefs such as in the afterlife that address death, it is popularly believed that certain meditative, contemplative, or spiritual states enable someone to transcend their own sense of self and such fears as may attend its loss. This may indeed occur, but whether it is a sustained state or transient makes a real difference here. The person better be sure to be in a transcendental state when the end comes.

In a show of unparalleled hubris, a group of high-tech billionaires has recently formed to solve the problem of death by declaring it ridiculous and vowing to do away with it. Having conquered the human economy with their gadgets and toys, they think they can unlock the secrets to the universe and undo one of its biological necessities. There appears, in fact, to be an entire movement of "life-extenders," "immortalists," and "longevity allies," comprised of health practitioners, scientists, technologists, and entrepreneurs, working to challenge human death. At least some of them realize there may be real implications if they succeed (such as who gets the fix when). Recent research on telomeres holds promise for extending life, but we may be a long way from achieving immortality.

In this regard, we may ask ourselves if living forever is even what we would want. Assuming aging could be arrested and bodies and minds maintained, we would be frozen in a kind of static social state (if others were also immortalized), which may not be a bad thing. But our particular skills and limitations would presumably not change much, unless technology also found a way to endow us beyond our natural abilities. In that case, how would society even cope with so much talent all at once?

Perhaps our attitude toward death represents not so much fear as regret about leaving life. In his farewell broadcast the famous television commentator Andy Rooney poignantly faced the future at 92 and said he wasn't happy about it [dying] at all. It was said that "[h]e loved his life," and that would surely explain his discontent. He died a month after retiring from a more than sixty-year career (word to the wise).

Then there are those who say they have no regrets about dying, that they have achieved all their life goals. I have heard this from a few friends and associates. I am tempted, but hesitate, to ask them what these goals are, that they could have fulfilled all of them and find nothing left, essentially, to live for. Charles Krauthammer, the well-known columnist who recently died, said in his farewell, facing terminal illness, "I leave this life with no regrets. It was a wonderful life — full and complete with the great loves and great endeavors that make it worth living. I am sad to leave, but I leave with the knowledge that I lived the life that I intended." No regrets, but sadness still. Life fulfilled, at least. And lived as desired. In the present situation where death still prevails, these are certainly all we can ask of life.

Aging

WHAT IS IT ABOUT aging that seemingly puts people into a mode of speaking, thinking, acting, and feeling? And is this any different from the way behavior is manifested in earlier life stages, which we disparage less?

We've all experienced the aging phenomenon in family members: restricted hours and early retirement; constant worries about all possible happenings; curmudgeonly attitudes toward others; compulsion to repeat the same stories from the past; and, unfortunately, increasing inability and unwillingness to navigate the world. Most of these traits appear even without the debilitating effects of dementia or stroke, which sadly aggravate them.

Of course, with aging eventually comes a slowing of the body's capacity for work and activity. Even without ailments or injuries seniors are prone to – such as arthritis and fractures – the body seems to decline significantly for most people sometime in the eighth decade (seventies). Seniors tend to be less adventurous or willing to go on excursions because they doubt their ability to cope with normal and unexpected obstacles. There are always exceptions, such as the octogenarian marathoners and mountain climbers, but they merely prove the rule.

This reluctance to foray into the world is associated with an increased fear of its dangers. Part of the fear comes from the wisdom of life experience, having seen so many things go wrong, so many accidents, and plans gone awry. With a less positive attitude dominant in the aging from loss of confidence in oneself and the world, a host of cautionary traits emerges: being careful and deliberate about every move (literal and figurative); worrying about executing upcoming events; nagging family members about preparing for future events and about all possible dangers in their lives; and talking about these worries to the exclusion of most else.

Essentially, the balance tips in later years from proactive to defensive motivations. Youth tends to be careless if not heedless of danger in order to fulfill its desires. Age tends to be excessively careful to protect itself and others from danger. Certainly, the defensiveness derives in part because age no longer has the urge to move forward, build, produce, and reproduce. In the throes of life's primary stages – procreation/family, career, exploration, achievement, and self-fulfilment – one is willing to tolerate considerable discomfort and pain. With most of life experience behind, such tolerance diminishes significantly. Older people are not known for being open to new, potentially challenging experiences, nor are they willing to sacrifice hard-earned comfort for a future unknown. Who can blame them, when they are no longer driven to go through the mill?

But what about the good traits of the aging – their wealth of experience and perspective, their concern for the youngest generations, their knowledge of the past and the workings of the world?

There is, in fact, a host of *positive* traits of the aging that may not be as prominent but deserve consideration and praise. These also include a capacity for kindness, generosity, and warmth and a level of understanding and wisdom derived from their life experience. The former qualities are manifested in the special relationship between the aging and their grandchildren. I well remember the love my maternal grandmother felt for me and the delight I experienced helping her make her old-world recipe of kreplach. As for the wisdom of age, smart seniors know when and how much to offer advice to their grown children and grandchildren. As always, the children (although grown) are more likely to resist such advice.

It is fair to ask if aging is any different from other life stages in having particular modes of behavior. The answer is clearly no: infancy, early youth, teenage, young adult, and middle age all have their types of behavior. In fact, we have already identified some key modes of the latter two, such as the drive to procreate and establish careers. These drives certainly result in common behaviors such as assertiveness, overconfidence or self-doubt, and preoccupation with self and one's own family. The teenage period is rife with behaviors that are the bane of parents, teachers, and law enforcement. We talk more forgivingly about early youth and infancy, but toddlers' behavior drives most parents nuts. In short, each life stage has its typical behaviors based on the person's physical and psychological condition at that age, and not all behaviors are any more attractive than those of the aging.

Then why do we tend to disparage aging more than all the others? In modern Western society, we certainly do. With the centric viewpoint being that of adulthood (young and middle-age), the other life stages are generally looked upon with benignity or noblesse oblige; not so the last stage, which irritates adults more than all the others.

The problem is that the aging are diminishing, not growing, and their unattractive traits tend to get worse rather than disappear, as those of toddlers and teens developmentally do. Once the defensive mode sets in, it doesn't reverse, and adult children can look forward to years of it. Seniors also show the rest of the population what is eventually in store for them as they age, and most people don't want to think about that. Even teens, who consider themselves ageless if not immortal, put "old people" in a separate mental place from the rest.

In fact, Western society has no place for the aging other than institutionalized living ("extended care," "assisted living," and nursing homes). They are given no productive place in society, being forced or encouraged to end their careers, and are currently seen as a huge financial liability. Seniors have had to create a place for themselves socially (through group activities like bridge and travel) and politically (through their association, AARP). Volunteer activities fill some seniors' days, sometimes quite productively; but as one senior told me long ago, if you aren't being paid, you aren't really considered of value. That our society is ageist is unmistakable.

I wish it weren't so, and we didn't look down on the aging, because we all get old if we are lucky. Even though I'm approaching that stage, I feel quite young and spry. Of course, I'm never irritable or fed up with the world; I never fuss about things unduly; and I've had only three debilitating health conditions this past year. But I know eventually I, too, will be considered among the aging and might exhibit some of its less attractive traits. Just put a four-inch lollipop in my mouth when that happens, please.

Health and Wealth

WHAT IS IT ABOUT health and wealth, that we don't appreciate them until we lose them?

We typically take good health for granted: when we have it for any length of time, we feel "normal" and accept it as the way things should be. Only someone who has recently been ill or injured or has overcome a sustained debilitating condition might reflect appreciatively on their current good health. The rest of us attend to other things, as we should, and don't constantly compare ourselves with a potentially worse physical condition that might limit our normal activities and aspirations.

Yet, we know that good health is indeed a grant of good fortune that is not guaranteed in life. Disease is rampant in the world, even in the developed one, and few go through life without many small maladies and a few larger ones. We will likely be felled by one, hopefully not until old age. The specter of serious and fatal illness hangs around society throughout history. Today in developed countries it is mostly about cancer and heart disease; in former times and in the developing world, the communicable diseases and plagues were, and continue to be, the central scare.

We are also happy to attend to our healthy lives rather than compare them with ill ones because illness is such a sink of time and attention (in addition to the discomfort, pain, and other debilitating conditions). Everything we take for granted in our healthy state becomes a conscious effort in an ill one. We have to work around a limitation or obstacle in order to do something that was habitual. Modern medicine brings its own set of add-ons, from endless appointments with numerous specialists to new technologies to understand to pharmacologies of uncertain benefit or genuine harm, all underlain by the maze of health insurance policies. While many medical advances have extended life and comfort, they are accompanied by bureaucratic and technological burdens that must be borne in compensatory time and effort.

What appears to be lack of gratitude for good health may, then, really be a form of conscious amnesia, a willingness to forget unpleasantness. It is telling, for example, how soon after recovering from an illness we can forget what it was like. This self-applied anesthetic enables us to move on, of course. For some it allows them to continue with dangerous behaviors like taking drugs or doing extreme sports, often bringing a reprise of the forgotten bad condition.

In general, a balanced attitude toward health may be a good thing. If we focused more on every moment of good health, we would likely become obsessed about losing it. This would make it difficult to carry out our lives. There is, of course, a happy medium here, where one can be cognizant of the value of good health so as to maintain it, but not stressed out about it. If youth are too much on the indifferent side, assuming they will always be healthy and invulnerable, older people are often too much on the obsessive side.

Despite the aphorism that there is nothing more important than your health, most of us focus instead on how much wealth we have. And here again, we generally don't appreciate what we have until we risk losing it. Except for the exceedingly wealthy, most people continue to want more, to aspire to more material trappings that elevate their status or match friends, neighbors, or celebrities. That this race to be rich produces little satisfaction has been well documented by writers over the ages and by the hollow lives it often produces in those so entrapped. It doesn't help that Western capitalist systems reward wealth by producing more of it for the wealthy, suggesting that there is never enough for the individual to be satisfied. (It also doesn't help that much of this wealth can be lost in a flash in the markets, feeding anxiety on top of dissatisfaction.)

One might be tempted to attribute the desire for more wealth to our modern, materialistic society. More traditional societies had their hierarchies of wealth, too, but most people were resigned if not contented to be in the economic class they were born to. This static vision of the past disguises, however, the fact that wealth was formerly much less abundant and available only to a few. So the proclivity to want more and not appreciate what one has is not necessarily a change in human heart. Rather, the desire for more wealth has become more universal over time as societies have accumulated wealth and distributed it more widely, making the opportunity to gain wealth available to many more people.

On the positive side, one could argue that dissatisfaction with one's current wealth is a necessary driver for individual initiative and societal progress. Where there is no hope for economic advancement or no desire to achieve it, people are not motivated to work harder, to be entrepreneurial, or to invent new ways to address market and social challenges. Such has been the West's criticism of communism as an economic system. In this view society makes every effort to encourage individuals' dissatisfaction with their economic status to goad them into gaining more wealth, but equally tries to deflect discontent that stems from economic inequality or perceived lack of equal opportunity.

In fact, complacency about health and dissatisfaction about wealth are two aspects of the same attitude that helps us function in our day-to-day lives. Good health is a given – though the more thoughtful understand that it is "God-given" – and we think about all we are capable of doing now rather than all we could *not* do without it. We *do*, however, think about all we do *not* have materially that we *could* have with more wealth, because this motivates us to do more to attain it. Only when fortune turns the other way in either case do we realize all we had and how valuable it was. For we are then in a different mode of living – trying to regain the gift of health or the wealth we had to live as we once did.

Aliens

WHAT IS IT ABOUT aliens of the extraterrestrial type that both fascinates and horrifies us? And if intelligent alien life were to show up, would humans change how they act and think?

We're not talking here about microbes scientists might find buried under miles of ice on Mars or in the rings of Saturn. No, these are actual *creatures* who act like us even though they may not look like us. We have seen them in the movies, in the pages of science fiction, and in our own imaginations. Although there has never been credible evidence of their existence, many people believe they exist and will eventually come to planet Earth.

It is easy to understand this conviction. It's a big universe out there, and we get lonely thinking about all the lifeless space. We do have our fellow hominids and our beloved canines, felines, and avians. But when things get existential, it's nice to have a companion at the top of the pecking order. The hope for cosmic companionship can be justified on the basis that, for all the miracles that created life on Earth, there must surely be a replication in some form elsewhere among the billions of galaxies.

Just what form this alien life might take constitutes the fascination. Our alien creations are never exactly like humans; some feature varies, whether it's a pointed ear lobe or a superior faculty. This makes sense from the perspective of how life evolved on Earth, where similar but not identical traits may be found in different species under similar conditions (the phenomenon of convergent evolution). We get more fascinated as the form of the alien becomes more alien, fundamentally different from ours, and the being's behavior unlike what we expect from ourselves.

This is where the horror comes in. Certainly, any form that appears grotesque to us – such as multiple "heads" or monstrous-looking bodies – puts us in a fight-or-flight mode, which is well-exploited by movies and fiction. The non-humanoid forms we imagine, such as dynamic blobs or gases, can be more horrifying, as they have no resemblance to ourselves and are typically impossible to fight or ward off. But it is ultimately not the form of the alien, but rather its motives, intentions, and powers, that cause us wonder or horror.

So often we imagine these alien motivations to be destructive toward us. Since the aliens have come to Earth first before we reached them, they are presumed to be of superior intellectual and technological powers. Typically, they come with the purpose of subjugating or destroying us. Curiously, if we consider the human capacity for moral behavior to be one of its highest evolutionary achievements, these superior aliens seem to have missed out on this development. Sometimes the story deals with this paradox by justifying an alien takeover on the grounds of human moral failure. But usually it's just a straight case of alien invasion and domination.

Like our terrestrial monster stories, which have an old lineage in human lore, aliens can be seen as a projection of what humans most fear about the world and about themselves. Humanoids are an obvious reflection of ourselves in partial disguise; the unusual traits represent characteristics we most fear or wish for ourselves, such as supernatural powers. Blobs and such are the epitome of what is scariest in our earthly world – organisms completely unlike ourselves or physical phenomena we cannot control. With extraterrestrial beings, however, there is no limit to the potential horror because they are not bound by earthly forms and experience. So the imaginative possibilities are endless, as are the fears that may result from them.

Like any dominant power, humans, who think they sit on top of the earthly biological hierarchy, are insecure about their status. Many alien stories speak to this unease by having these supposedly superior beings come and displace us. But let's imagine what might happen if we were visited by aliens of high intelligence and moral character who are not intent merely on subjugating us. Might this change our outlook on the world and ourselves and fundamentally alter our behavior ever after?

I admit I sometimes wish for this to happen: a visitation from another world with benign intent to root out human evil and destruction by example and benevolent authority. Seen from afar, humans have created a chaotic world where so many things violate our own ideals and norms. Poverty, crime, war, violence, waste, and destruction all bedevil our societies and fall short of what most of them preach. Wouldn't it be wonderful to have a truly "humane" alien group set us straight for once and for all in our history? This *deus ex machina* is, of course, not only woefully wishful but also a sorry excuse for our failure to be what we should be. But it surely appeals in the face of all that goes on in this world at our hands.

Let's assume a higher alien authority merely visits and leaves without directly re-ordering our lives. Unlike most alien stories, they have no need to stay and dominate; perhaps they know that merely by appearing they will have a salutary effect on us. For I do believe that such an occurrence would rock the human world to its core. We would no longer consider ourselves the ultimate life form of the universe, with the privilege that seems to convey. We would have seen how superior beings deal with themselves and others, even when they presumably have the power to wreak evil upon us. Consequently, we would see everything we do and that we have created in a different light, warts and all, and be motivated to make them better.

Consider the effect of the landing of humans on the moon in 1969 and the picture of "Earthrise" taken the year before from lunar orbit. Yes, the Vietnam War continued along with many bad things on Earth. But the perspective of the moon visit and the view of our contained, blue world against the barren lunar surface enlightened many to the preciousness of life on Earth and the danger of our accelerating destruction of the environment. Soon after, not entirely by coincidence, the U.S. government formed an agency to protect the environment and passed a series of laws to reduce the rampant pollution choking our resources at that time. More fundamentally, the lunar perspective gave graphic meaning to the concept developing then of a Spaceship Earth of which are all an inescapable part.

If the moon landing and perspective were epochal events – deriving from our own actions upon a familiar planetary body – how much more significant would be the visit of alien beings from a remote extrasolar world. The entire front page of *The New York Times* was dedicated to the lunar landing; if aliens came here, its banner headline might take up the entire page. That's how much of an impact the event would have. History would be re-written from that day on, and our perspective would change on all before.

But perhaps I wax too optimistic. As of this writing, the only "aliens" we know about are foreign nationals, strange life forms on Earth, and bizarre humans among us. Our ufologist friends might beg to differ, but so far no higher life form has come along to the best of our knowledge. We seem, indeed, to be alone in the universe for all practical purposes. Extraterrestrial aliens might best be viewed as an expression of our terrestrial existence: we create them to fill a void and provide zest to our mundane lives. It may be just as well, for there is no assurance a real alien would not terrorize us, as we sometimes do to other humans and species on Earth.

Misperception

WHAT IS IT ABOUT human perception, that it can be inaccurate much of the time? Is this a distinctly human trait or something shared by the sentient animal kingdom? And is there any advantage conferred by our misperception?

A few examples suffice to illustrate the issue. On the auditory side, there is the well-known distortion that occurs when a sentence is quietly spoken from one individual to another around a large circle. The final version often bears little resemblance to the initial one, as people either do not hear correctly what they are told or reinterpret it in the re-telling. On the visual side, there is the inevitable discrepancy in how different people relate the same event they witnessed. When testimony is given in court under oath, credible witnesses may portray a scene quite differently. The judicial system provides for cross-examination of witnesses to delve into the details and potential misperceptions to ferret out the truth. Even in regard to non-crisis events, a willing observer who intends to be accurate often is not, and one person's rendition of events may differ from another's. This can all happen in good faith, when people attempt to report exactly what they perceive.

Part of what is involved here is certainly deficient physical perception of auditory and visual stimuli. Humans are generally not good listeners, as we seem to have difficulty focusing for any length of time on what other people say. Even before the current age of multiple distractions (such as from smartphones), people were easily distracted, as can be seen from old photographs of audiences "listening" to speeches. Observe a pair or group of people in conversation and see how much attention anyone normally gives to the speaker. Visually humans are somewhat more focused but still rather limited in what they actually see. We call someone "observant" if, unlike most people, the person actually picks up on details in a scene. Moreover, perhaps even more than with hearing, deficient eyesight plagues many people and can blur the details quite literally.

Beyond our physical limitations, however, human perception cannot avoid being colored by our minds. Our perception of events, objects, and people is influenced by what we think about them, what is already on our minds, and what we want to believe. In each case the sensory information is processed through these filters, which select and emphasize certain data and even distort some of it. This process occurs because our minds are preconditioned by our thinking to perceive things in certain ways. Contrary impressions may still come through, but the dissonance requires additional processing.

As a result, our senses can configure experience in specific, individualized ways. Even simple objects seen at a distance can be interpreted as very different things by different people. More so a sequence of events: the very order of actions can be recalled differently, depending on what was most salient to the observer; and the nature of the actions and people involved may be seen as negative, neutral, or positive depending on preconceptions. If we are favorably disposed to the actors, we are more likely to interpret what they do favorably, and vice versa. That is why jurors are vetted carefully with regard to their own experience with the particular issues involved in a trial. That is also a reason why minorities are arrested falsely more often than majority races, and why the former's actions or even just their presence may appear suspicious without any basis in fact.

It isn't just prejudice that shapes our perceptions. Our mind interprets sensory impressions through various categories based largely on experience and knowledge. What is meaningful to one person may be mysterious to another. For example, a sword and television screen would each look different to a medieval person than to a modern person. The sword to a medieval person is a fearsome weapon laden with immediate experience, to us today merely a relic or ornament; a television screen to a medieval person would be seen as a flat board of strange material and inexplicable purpose, but to us it is a gateway to many vicarious experiences. Entire philosophies and psychological theories have been developed to thus explain human perception. We need only appreciate here that what we perceive must necessarily align with what we can categorically understand.

Our everyday moods and thoughts also influence our perceptions. Sometimes when I am thinking about someone or something, I may interpret what I see in my immediate environment in relation to that person or thing. A stranger far down the street might initially look like that person, or I might "recognize" an otherwise undecipherable object in the woods as the object I was considering. Moods may alter perception by their selectivity and filtering. A melancholy mood may see more gray in the day, an upbeat mood, emerging sunshine.

Perhaps most powerful in influencing perception is what we want to believe. This relates to our preconceptions and prejudices but also to our hopes, desires, and wishes. Not only does our perception select those data that align with our feelings, but it also bends them, sometimes nearly to the breaking point, to fit the desired view. In this way perception acts both like a prism filtering what we see or hear and like gravity forcing what we see into the desired (if distorted) configuration. Nowhere does this happen more pathetically than with the lovelorn, who desperately see in any non-negative reaction of their loved one a reciprocal feeling toward themselves. This also occurs with those attending an ill person, when any slight change may be seen as significant improvement – only to be dashed by the doctor's dispassionate reading of the instruments. In these and many other situations, our beliefs and desires inevitably color our perception of events.

The well-known if controversial Rorschach Test uses differential perception of a fixed set of random patterns to help diagnose personality traits. Although the ten inkblot images used in the test do not strictly represent any person or object, subjects are asked to describe what they "see" in them. They are all symmetrical, disorganized (I am giving away my own personality here) images that look variously like faces, animals, reproductive organs, or such, according to the most popular responses. Although attributing particular personality traits from responses to these images may be dubious, the process involved certainly demonstrates how our perception of the same object can vary from individual to individual and how we project on external objects meanings that we hold within.

It should, of course, be acknowledged that human perception does a pretty good job overall relating to the world and interpreting it correctly for daily functioning. For the most part we recognize other people and objects correctly, and we don't run into walls as a rule. What is remarkable is that despite these successes, we still misperceive things more often than we think. Humans may not be alone in this respect, however. An astute observer of wildlife will occasionally see an animal have a mishap based on faulty perception or go after an object that was not actually what it thought. We see this also with our domesticated friends, who are generally quite shrewd in understanding our ways but occasionally mistake an object we carry as a treat. I would guess, however, that humans display instances of misperception more frequently than wild animals because evolution has more effectively and ruthlessly weeded out the susceptibility for misperception among the latter.

Since evolution shows little tolerance for maladaptive behavior, we might conversely ask whether human misperception confers any advantages for us. On its face the answer is plainly no: there is no necessary benefit to misconstruing what we see or hear. In fact, the opposite would likely be true, since we might get into real trouble misperceiving an enemy as a friend or reaching for a stick that is really a snake. But, more deeply, the question might rather be whether those faculties that contribute to our misperception do not also confer advantages that override the deficiencies they cause. Specifically, the human capacity to think about things, to recognize images and patterns, and to imagine conditions beyond the immediate one may make us more prone to misperception than other animals. But these very traits have also enabled us to develop unparalleled communicative faculties, to create culture, and to invent technologies that have (for the most part) promoted the survival of the human species.

This is not to say that misperception is a necessary result of mental activity and imagination. Certainly our limited sensory abilities play a role by providing latitude in interpreting what we see and hear. But our active imaginations as well as our categorical and conceptual thinking also come into play. We should celebrate these abilities that have so enriched our lives, even though they occasionally trip us up or deceive us. Being aware of this duality can help us manage the down side to foster a truer, more insightful perception of the world overall.

By Things Possessed

WHAT IS IT ABOUT our possessions that makes them so hard to do without? Why are we so different from other animals in this regard, and why do humans vary in their need for possessions?

All humans except monastics and Henry David Thoreau carry with them a host of things they consider essential. Some of these may even date back to childhood, but most are collected as a person matures and makes a life of their own. A typical portfolio of possessions ranges widely from daily necessities like clothes and toiletries to hobby and sports paraphernalia to memorabilia from the person's past. All of them are guarded zealously from incursion by other family members or roommates.

Our concern here is not with houses or places in which to live, but everything else of a material nature people possess and bring with them when they move. All animals need a place to live, and many build their own homes in the form of nests, burrows, cocoons, or other structures. Corals and termites may make the most elaborate houses outside of humans, while other animals, such as many types of fish or ungulates like deer, make do with sheltering niches in their environment rather than building their own. But only humans bring with them a hoard of other things to fill up their homes.

Some other animals do have possessions besides a nest or house, but almost always these are directly related to food or survival, such as avian or rodent caches of nuts, spider webs woven for prey, or ant farms for food. Otherwise, animals are free to move whenever they need to, re-creating their homes and re-establishing territories for habitation, food, and reproduction. Humans cannot function this way, starting with the clothes they need in almost all climes, tools for gathering and preparing food and water, and articles used for body care and sanitation. Our basic possessions are essential to our survival because humans are built without the outer layer (fur, feathers, scales, exoskeletons, etc.) that enables other animals to survive outside or the built-in tools (e.g., claws, beaks, very sharp teeth) with which to forage or capture food.

In our "civilized" state, however, we have added on innumerable, mostly superfluous objects to supposedly enhance our well-being. These include expansive wardrobes, personal vehicles, telecommunication devices (television, radio, computer, phones and smartphones, etc.), and leisure equipment. In addition – and this may be uniquely human – we carry with us things that are surrogates for our identity and self-image, which are likely to harken from our past yet stay with us for a long time. These may include school and university diplomas, photographs, souvenirs, jewelry, items associated with another person, books, letters, etc. We may cling to these personal possessions with a tenacity equal to or exceeding our hold on true necessities. Identity is, after all, a powerful force, as is our personal history.

In addition, many discretionary or luxury items to which the developed world has become accustomed play a duplicate role in defining ourselves. People buy certain cars and clothes for their style and to make a statement; they may engage in particular leisure activities, including sports, fitness, and travel, partly for the image they project. All the relevant possessions can become very important to an individual. That is why modern humans have such difficulty distinguishing between true necessities and things that are nice to have. When a basic need becomes stymied, such as access to heat or water, we are often shocked as we are jarred back into the realm of genuine necessity.

Although most people in more affluent countries have a considerable number of possessions, the amount each individual possesses can range widely depending on a number of factors, including age, wealth, and personality. As people mature into adulthood and take actual possession of their things, they begin to accumulate more based on their experiences. Over time this process can create quite a heap, especially if a family is involved, although when people get much older they tend to shed some of them. A person's wealth also affects their stock. Whether it involves cars, clothes, leisure equipment, or luxury items like art, wealthy people tend to have more stuff because they can afford to satisfy every want.

Aside from these baselines factors, personality combined with life history plays the biggest role in determining a person's portfolio of possessions. From the youngest age many need some thing to provide security (when mother is absent), such as a blanket or lovey (stuffed animal or doll). These anchor objects often continue to be needed in adulthood but in other forms, like one's wallet, car, or sewing machine. The degree to which one holds to anchor objects and their number reflect one's personality, with less secure people on the more intense and higher end of the range. The type of anchor objects retained by more sensitive types tends to be more personal and idiosyncratic as well. Added to the anchor objects may be a number of keepsakes reflecting nostalgia for the past or losses of family, friends, or ways of life. Such memory objects reflect an individual's feeling about his or her past and attitude about change and loss.

A person's experience growing up in their natal family certainly affects their attachment to things. How their parents and other siblings relate to their things obviously has an influence. If a parent is particularly adamant in terms of saving or discarding things, the child may react in kind or in reverse. The individual's place in the sibling pecking order also factors in, since those at the lower end may get less than their fair share and have a greater need for things to compensate. In broader terms, the family's overall wealth determines how many and what kind of objects may be available, along with the value placed on particular items.

As adults people also acquire beliefs or ideologies that may affect their attitude toward possessions. They may have a sense of personal or family history that would prompt them to save older things, such as photographs or jewelry. Conversely, those who don't ever look back would likely shed or pass off objects from the family's more distant past. Also, some people have a strong sense of thrift and aversion to waste, while others are less concerned about these matters. For the former, objects may be retained because they can be used later or in a different way, according to the adage that pollution [junk] is a resource out of place. Attics, basements, garages, and barns may become stores of objects in accordance with this viewpoint.

This brings us to the dichotomy between hoarders and chuckers, representing the two extremes of those who tend to save things and those who tend to discard them. Hoarding can become pathological when everything is kept as if valuable and the person's abode becomes so cluttered it impedes normal functioning. To my knowledge there is not a comparable pathology for chuckers, although I have seen some in action be very wasteful and take a manic glee in throwing out perfectly good things. Moreover, even chuckers may have a significant number of prized possessions they consider highly valuable – when they own them.

In disclosure, I am more on the hoarder end, in part because I hate to waste usable things and in part for personality reasons (last born, sensitive to loss, etc.). I've carried around things from early childhood, notes and notebooks from high school, college, and graduate school, and many mementos and keepsakes. While I can get into a chucker mode and even downsize when necessary, I always worry I will discard something I will later regret. I justify myself as a mild hoarder by identifying with the Yankee tradition of thrift. Having children, even if they are grown, also provides an excuse on the shaky notion they will care some day about their parents' past and their antiquated possessions.

Whatever the differences among individuals and their causes, humans have certainly accumulated a hoard of material possessions, growing like our landfills as society increases in wealth. New storage-for-rent buildings spring up across the landscape, even in remoter areas, to take all the things people can't keep in their houses but can't relinquish. We have certainly gone far beyond what is necessary for our survival and welfare as humans. Many of these supernumeraries may in fact have intrinsic value to the individual, but others undoubtedly clutter our lives and impede our focus on the essential. Trips and vacations, where we pack only what we need, fulfill our fantasy of getting free of things. But we wouldn't want to come home and find our most important possessions gone. We are truly, as humans in the modern age, by our things possessed.

Unmoved

WHAT IS IT ABOUT moving, that it is considered so stressful to almost everyone?

I'll acknowledge at the outset that I don't understand all the fuss about moving one's home from one place to another. Most animals do this frequently, and human nomads seem to do just fine. Not counting my rootless university years (when I moved nine times), I have moved eight times in my adulthood, and each has been more pleasant than the last. I've learned to perfection the techniques of packing and moving, and I've come to realize how enjoyable the process can be.

Yet most people stress out before, during, and after a move. It seems widely accepted that moving is one of the most stressful events in life, along with losing a loved one, losing one's job and livelihood, divorce, and such. One authoritative online source opines that "[e]veryone hates moving." Clearly, not everyone does, but even if I'm the only one who doesn't, I am confident I can elucidate the joys of moving to convince everyone else. As always, we seek here to look below the surface to understand what is really going on – what it is about.

The answer is not, as some claim, that moving disrupts our routines. All of us fantasize breaking free of routine and living on an island away from pesky work, family, and friends. Nor is moving stressful because it involves change, which most people supposedly can't tolerate. That's really a canard – everyone loves change, especially when it involves so much pleasure. No, these are the usual stereotypical beliefs that get circulated widely and acquire value only through repetition, not accuracy.

As with everything in life, one has to see moving in the right way. What appears to be difficult physically and emotionally can actually be a boon to body and spirit. The following is just a sample of the good aspects of moving that are often overlooked: you can leave behind annoying neighbors, obnoxious co-workers, and friends who talk all the time about their children; you can throw out your family's most valuable possessions and leave unfixed all those problems in the old house; you get daily exercise lifting boxes and furniture and spend pleasant hours on the phone or computer changing your address; you can chase after the mail the post office doesn't forward correctly; and, not least, you get to spend a lot of money you didn't know you had. All these warrant a closer look to show just how beneficial moving really is.

Living in one place for any length of time invariably puts you in touch with people you cannot stand but cannot escape. While unsavory people can be found anywhere, the ones who cling are most often around your home or office. By the law of averages, if you have bad apples to deal with in these places, your next move will put you in contact with better ones. You can kiss goodbye to dowdy Miss Jill next door or underhanded Ralph at work. Garrulous Kathy, who regales you frequently with her children's latest crises, will also be left far behind.

And when you move, you have sanction – on the excuse of downsizing – to get rid of not only your own possessions, but also those of the kids and your spouse. There can be no more cathartic feeling, especially when chucking someone else's stuff. You have to target the most prized possessions of the family, since these are held the longest and cause the most clutter. That this will get a rise out of everyone makes it especially tantalizing and salutary: the anger that ensues will help cleanse everyone's spirit in time for the family's move.

No doubt you are a conscious homeowner who tries to maintain your place in good repair. But any house has myriad small problems that never get completely fixed. The list, being endless, can drive anyone crazy; but when you move, all that goes away! Sure, you may have to disclose some of them in settlement, and you would anyway, being an honest person. But those little but annoying things – like the toilet roll holder that keeps coming loose, sending the paper into the bowl; the furnace that sometimes doesn't go on in the dead of winter; the basement that floods in every storm – these small matters, as I said, you can just let ride and have the new owner deal with. Again, chances are that the house you move into won't have such problems, because everything looked great when you secured it.

Of course, there's a crisis in America today with lack of fitness, and moving is just the thing to address the problem. If you have already broken your new year's resolution to exercise more, just decide to move this year. You'll find that, notwithstanding the young men you hired to move all your things out of town, there will be plenty of opportunity for you to pull out your back and crush your toes while packing and unpacking. These risks are more than worthwhile considering the fine exercise you'll sustain moving around boxes and furniture as you prepare for the big day and figure out what to do with your overload on the other end.

Then there's the joy of changing your address scores of times for all the institutions you deal with, not to say all the friends and relatives you have to inform. I know it would be easier if there were a central registry so you could change your address just once for everyone. But that would keep you from the pleasure of performing this repetitive task. You'd miss out talking with Charlotte in insurance and Jim in banking and Rudolph in motor vehicles. Moreover, having a single place to change your address may not help the situation; doing so with the Postal Service only guarantees that your mail will not come either to your current or to your new home, but instead will cycle endlessly between them until it frays into fiber.

Some may find the cost of moving a major problem and cause for chagrin. True, with moving trucks and labor, recyclers and junk haulers, packaging material, and other associated expenses like eating out all the time, the bill will be so high you'll have to search through your savings to pay for it. But the money there was only getting a few cents interest every month anyway, and that just made balancing your bank books difficult. Besides, you'll have the satisfaction of transferring your remaining wealth to the small mobsters who own moving companies instead of the Wall Street crooks who own your bank.

In sum, moving really isn't so stressful after all. In fact, it involves myriad pleasures one cannot derive elsewhere. When people commiserate with those who are moving and complacently stay put, they forego an unmatched opportunity to refresh their lives and leave the baggage behind. I trust that if they read this piece, they will see the light and order movers to come take them – anywhere – next week.

Choices

WHAT IS IT ABOUT life choices, that they can so affect the course of our lives? How much do our choices really alter our lives, and what else influences their course?

I think about the key decisions of my life and how it may have evolved if I had made different choices about career, lifestyle, relationships, and critical situations. This is no Walter Mitty exercise fantasizing a wannabe life, but rather consideration of real choices I grappled with and paths I decided to take, or not. My parents had a particular notion about which occupation I should pursue. I wrestled with their desire and ultimately chose something quite different. While I never really regretted not doing what they wanted, I have had doubts about what I chose, starting with my college major. Repeated thought experiments trying out alternative choices have somewhat assuaged my doubts, but not entirely.

It should be acknowledged that the topic of this essay assumes a certain level of privilege that allows for such choices in life. I and many others in the developed world have been fortunate to be able to choose among various occupations and make other lifestyle choices. Those in economically distressed circumstances or in other countries with little opportunity or freedom have to get by as best they can with what is available. Their choices are much more limited, if they have any at all; or they may be unsavory ones, such as between poverty and illicit activity. Having the freedom and opportunity to make life choices may be a weighty responsibility, but it is also a tremendous gift not everyone today shares and most of our forebears never had.

For much of human history an individual's place in society was mostly ordained by necessity or circumstance. In subsistence cultures there was little opportunity for occupations other than obtaining food and securing the community. Specialties sprang up as society developed and expanded its functions and services. In the modern developed world, many diverse occupations have been created in response to industrialization, specialization, and technological advancement. Until recently, parents had considerable say about what career their children (primarily male) would pursue. In the West, at least, these strictures have been lifted along with the liberation of women freely to pursue careers. In recent decades we have witnessed an entirely new group of specialties that has emerged with the advent of the computer and digital age. While not everyone gets to share in these diverse choices, the opportunity overall is greater than at any other time in history.

Each decision we make about the big choices – occupation, mate, place to live, etc. – certainly does have significant ramifications for our lives. At the least, one's way of living (lifestyle) can be very different depending on one's occupation, in terms of both daily activity and the possessions afforded by income received. Geographical location also affects us through its climate, demography, population density, and innate culture. Relationships rate very highly in influence, with longer-term ones, particularly marriage, generally most significant. The adage that ninety percent of one's happiness (or misery) comes from the person one marries may be an exaggeration, but it underscores the significance of the choice. After all, such a long-term relationship involves constant togetherness and typically offspring to raise jointly, so it definitely affects one's life significantly.

It is, nonetheless, a fair question to ask how much these decisions affect us deep down. Would we be a fundamentally different person depending on the occupation we choose, the place we live, the person we marry? In many ways the answer is no: we remain fundamentally the same in character and personality and the issues implicit to each. But that does not mean our experience of life does not fundamentally vary depending on these choices. Furthermore, because our character and personality are to some extent shaped by our experience and grow with it, our temperament may change somewhat with the choices we make. We have all seen – if not personally experienced – the transformation in state-of-mind that can come over someone as their life situation changes, for better or for worse.

These big decisions of our own are not, however, the only significant influences on our lives. As discussed elsewhere in this volume,[14] much of what occurs in our lives is beyond our direct control, and seemingly chance occurrences (so-called fate) can significantly affect our lives. One is born into a particular situation – family, country, class, demographic, period, etc. – and this is the "hand" one has to play with and the context in which one makes choices. Our decisions may thus be bounded, limited, buffeted, and altered in specific directions. But this is true regardless of the choices we make, in that there will always be external forces shaping our lives. While some life courses may be more subject to fate and unforeseen circumstances, for most of us these unknowns can be considered a kind of random constant that cannot be planned around. Hence, we make decisions based on the situation we know and can best foresee.

Calculating the actual import of one's major decisions can be tricky business, with a risk in either under- or overestimating their magnitude. Personality plays a role here, since easy-going types tend to take such decisions more casually than more intense types, who may analyze each one as if it determines their entire future. For those who attend college, the first big decision of their lives may be which to apply to and then which one to select; for others, it may be which occupation to enter or get training in. Parents need to remind adolescents that their entire life need not, in fact, depend on such choices. Equally revealing is the choice of mate. While most people fall into relationships, when it comes to deciding on long-term ones such as marriage the decision-making gets more serious and telling. There are some who remain casual even about marriage, but most approach it with more gravity. On the other hand, there is danger in believing that this one choice will completely "solve" a person's life and resolve their other issues or problems.

Such conflation of decisions is not uncommon, particularly as regards emotional matters. One would like to believe that resolving one problem will resolve another – that, for example, finding the right mate will help clarify one's identity and calling. Adolescents and young adults may be most prone to this pitfall, but all of us at any

---

[14] In the essay, "Optimistic Fatalism."

stage can become thus wishful. Bringing extraneous factors into our own decisions does not necessarily make them relevant or resolve what is behind them. Talking with a third party, professional or friend, often helps us sort out these factors.

In the grand confusion of my early adulthood, I had to confront all these challenges in making decisions about my life ahead. Parental wishes for a particular career lumbered against my personal preferences, which I followed. On the relationship side I had, like most of us, a sufficient number of trials. But ultimately I have been fortunate in marriage – thank you, Rebecca! – and have the blessing of fine grown children. Added now is a choice that harkens back to my youthful dreams, to write. I hope the reader finds pleasure in the product, which I guarantee is not conflated with anything else in my life.

Love and Affection

WHAT IS IT ABOUT love and affection that two living beings can feel so positively toward each other beyond biological (sexual) attraction? How does this type of feeling differ from other natural attractive forces such as the gravitational attraction between two objects, and how essential is it to the world?

Biological attraction is mysterious enough, although it asserts itself tautologically as imperative to our very existence: without it, we would not be here to question how it arises. Whatever its actual mechanism, no species would continue unless some form of reproductive process had evolved in it. We know that certain chemicals activate the brain in higher animals to engage in sexual activity. Presumably these chemicals and neural responses evolved as each species did.

Love and affection certainly reinforce reproductive urges, and evolutionary psychology holds that they also evolved to ensure reproductive and child-rearing success. The companion essay to this one ("Love and Disaffection") acknowledges this. But something more is often involved in human love and that of some other species. The strength of feelings, the potential for sacrifice, can go much beyond what is needed to ensure the procreative bond and continuing child care. This is seen also in non-romantic love and affection such as between close friends, who do not generally play a role in propagating the species. It must be acknowledged, then, that love and affection have some life of their own, some motivating force, beyond just maintaining the species.

This force that draws people together and stimulates love and affection for each other is indeed wondrous. Nature has created out of matter something that is not only animate, creative, thoughtful, and functional, but also capable of being attracted to other living beings. This is no necessary result; our science fiction and fantasy writers have delivered many plausible scenarios where love is lacking in alien beings. Procreation can, as in *Brave New World*, be engineered and managed clinically by society. Instead, we humans and a number of animal species on Earth seem capable of going beyond the material into the realm of what we call the heart. Of course, the latter is a figure of speech (technically, a metonymy), since the heart probably has little to do with the actual feelings of love and affection activated in our nervous and endocrinal systems except when directed to pump harder. No matter – we are blessed to have these feelings, wherever they reside in us.

The phenomenon of love and affection between two living beings has a kind of parallel in the physical universe in the force of gravity. Any two objects with mass are attracted to each other and will move toward each other in the absence of restraining forces. Unlike love and affection, gravity is indiscriminate in its application, since it depends only on the masses of the two objects and their distance from each other. Love and affection, of course, generally depend on the particular people or animals involved, although there seems to be an innate potential for love and affection that provides for their expression in specific cases. Only with magic potions, as in *A Midsummer's Night Dream*, or with someone truly lovelorn will these feelings attach to most any object or person.

Both love and attraction and gravity work in mysterious, as yet unknown ways. Science can describe the workings of gravity and precisely measure and predict its force through Newton's equation. But no one understands how gravity actually works – how two detached objects, sometimes far distant from each other, can exert a physical force on one another. Various theories and hypotheses have been developed to explain it, including quantum gravity and general relativity, where such things as gravitons (massless particles) and gravitational waves (distortions of spacetime) "mediate" or convey the force of gravity. The Nobel laureate Edward Purcell once said in a lecture that he finds the repulsive force (such as in electromagnetism) bizarre, whereas attraction is commonplace, with our refrigerator door closing by itself as an example. I find both the attractive and the repulsive force equally puzzling. As a human, however, I find love and affection to be entirely natural, along with their opposite (in appropriate cases), even though the mechanics by which they function also remain unknown (lovitons and affect waves, perhaps?).

Without gravity much of our known universe would fall apart and would have evolved very differently. Do love and affection play a similar role in the animal world? Popular culture tells us so, with sayings like, "Love is everything," "Love makes the world go 'round," "Love conquers all," and "Love is all you need." Of course, underlying these expressions is "romantic" love, which certainly makes the animate world go around, for without reproduction animals would not continue to exist. But, as suggested earlier, there is more to these sayings than sex or the feelings that propel it.

Admittedly, adages tend to exaggerate a truth to drive home the point, and these are no different. One can't seriously claim that love and affection matter more than anything else and are the only important aspects of life. People vary in the importance they attach to emotions and emotional connections, with some valuing love and affection highly and others, often more practical and unemotional types, minimizing them. There is a danger, too, in elevating love too much, since it is a very powerful, enveloping emotion which can be unrequited or turn negative. But the human world – and, I suspect, the experience of many of our animal brethren – would be fundamentally different were we not to experience love and affection at all.

Because of its intensity it is easy to extol the joys of romantic love despite the suffering that may ensue. Love other than the romantic kind and affection also contribute positively to our lives. Think of the warm feelings one has for close friends and the pleasure of being in their company. Think of the special feelings one has for one's loved ones, over and beyond those necessary to ensure procreation and successful child-rearing. Understand too that one's feelings in these contexts are usually reciprocated or at least appreciated at some level. Without these emotions we would be bereft of some of the most valuable aspects of life.

Unlike romantic love, this kind of love and affection can apply universally. One may love and feel affection toward someone much older or younger, children, animals, and even plants and inanimate things. The potential for universality resembles gravity, but in actual application each individual feels love and affection only for certain living beings or objects. Conversely, only certain people or things provoke the opposite emotion of dislike in anyone. Almost everyone and everything seem to be in someone's positive orbit, however, lending credence to the saying that love is everything.

The beauty of love and affection derives not only from their universality but also from the selflessness that underlies them. Romantic love is almost always expressed as desire and need, sometimes to the point of demand; the other kind of love and affection are usually mutually given and not driven primarily by need. Where need becomes paramount in a relationship, love and affection become subordinate or diminished. In fact, nothing other than betrayal can compromise a friendship more than one person's becoming selfishly dependent on another. The other person may still feel love and affection, but the mutuality that is the foundation of the relationship is gone.

It may seem peculiar to compare love and affection to gravity. But, like celestial orbs, we organisms need something to hold us together emotionally. After all, it's a big world out there, and it can be pretty lonely considering our small place in it. The wonderful feelings of attraction and giving of which we are capable make life tolerable, livable, and at best joyous and rewarding. Love and affection enable us to come together with other bodies we feel aligned with. They endow our lives with an extraordinary additional force.

Gone

WHAT IS IT ABOUT the loss of loved ones, that we feel not only grief but that a part of us is lost forever? Can we ever get over such loss, and does doing so devalue the love we felt? If not "forgotten," how much should we reasonably "remember"?

***

HPW 1944-2002. She was four years older and treated me with all the maternal instinct she possessed. She grew up in a different world by time and position, closer to the parents and too close to mother. They evolved like two vines intertwining around each other, breeding conflict along with love and support.

She was precocious in every mental and emotional way, head of the class at private school, adversary of pretentious, ignorant teachers. Adolescence inflamed an already volatile personality, and some health problems ensued. She attended a fine college, followed by a succession of degrees in the humanities, with medieval and Chaucer specialties, her work lauded by leading experts for its innovative, cross-disciplinary analysis.

She taught for many years at another fine liberal arts college, offering not only her specialties but also multidisciplinary courses in film, women's studies, and even pornography (a homework assignment in which got her undesired notoriety). She was beloved by the many students whose work she assiduously reviewed and commented on, to the detriment of her research. But she still got tenure, a longer road than her brilliance deserved.

Her work was paramount, even as serious health problems mounted and became part of her way of life. She sent me her publications along with her medical reports. The tie to mother stayed strong throughout, with trips together while their health allowed. She died after years of illness and multiple hospitalizations. Her students were shocked and grief-stricken when they returned from summer break to the news.

She nurtured me in my youth, emotionally and intellectually. She was the guardian angel of my humanistic interests and helped me select courses at college in those fields. Beneath her brusque, almost misanthropic exterior always throbbed a child's heart. She wished for so much more in life, fundamentally idealistic, but became realistic and even cynical. I saw her seldom after she left for college, with several years passing between visits at times. Yet, her loss felt like a limb of mine had been lopped off.

***

PJB 1950-1996. I first saw her in the university library archives where she worked. A smile of true inner warmth overtook a nervous expression as we met. We frequented the coastline of the Sound she so loved, the woods, the Greek pizzerias.

She was a true daughter of New England – thrifty, reserved, stoic, honest, and selfless. She awakened me to the inner beauties of the place, the love of history and indigenous architecture. Her mother's home where she lived was full of antiques and her youthful paintings.

She went down South for graduate work in architectural history, then worked in historic preservation to protect vernacular forms. She objected to the gentrification taking hold in inner cities then and its effect on urban life. She contributed significant works in her field.

Years later she was stricken. She had begun painting again, and continued for five years with marvelous creations, ever more experimental and spiritual. She had several public art shows, written up in the papers. Her mother brought her back for hospice, and I went up to see her the day before she died. The marshes along the Sound she loved spread out just beyond where she lay, and again where she was buried.

Her paintings were her children, and I received several of them, carrying forward her quiet but intense vision. As a mutual friend said, she will never be forgotten, at least by us. But now that her mother and relatives are gone, I wonder about that, and know she deserved much better.

***

C-B 1988-2013. He came into my life through someone else, and we bonded immediately. Like the Alps I once lived in, my attachment to him grew deeper over time. He trusted me more than anyone else and sought my protection when needed, but otherwise he made clear who was in charge.

Early on he awakened my interest in animate nature, which he brought into the house through his natural behavior. I became a birder and balanced my interest in the physiography of Earth with renewed fascination for its patina of life. His songs, calls, and occasional screams mixed with the noises of the children. Frequent arias ten minutes or longer added to an already musical household.

He communicated in other unmistakable ways as well. A gentle touch of a favorite hanging bell signified acknowledgment of your presence or agreement with your move or speech; the same pendant could get wacked around wickedly to express annoyance or unmet needs. Long periods sitting in a favorite dish could occasionally result in territorial attacks if disturbed.

He knew how to enjoy himself and how to get repose. Except near the end, sitting in the sun was a favorite, replete with nibbles at the sunbeams. Evening shut him down, and window sills became preferred quieting areas where he countenanced no disturbance and resisted all bedtime appeals.

He took ill suddenly overnight after a near-manic post-Thanksgiving dinner interacting engagingly with the family. Several days later he died. I was devastated. I combed the wooded hills disconsolate the next day, and repeatedly interrogated myself how I might have averted his end. My zest for life, which he catalyzed, deflated. I couldn't listen to music for half a year. The ensuing years have lessened the pain, which I don't want to reopen, and this makes me feel a little like I have abandoned him, though I think of him, like the others, often.

***

We will never forget, but we do move on. We remember at appropriate times such as their anniversaries, at times we set by ritual, and when something day-to-day reminds us of them. To do more could impinge on our lives in ways they would not have desired. Our continuing remembrance if not grief is testament both to them and to our love for them. It may die with us, as it has with all preceding generations, but it is a love we hold fast for as long as we live. It is a balm for the loss we feel permanently.

Being and Fear Of

WHAT IS IT ABOUT being alive that it can be both sublime and frightful? Can we adjust this balance, and how do we manage each?

Our senses convey both beauty and pain. This glorious world made beautiful by nature, sunlight, and air bathes our senses if we allow it. Each phase of each day in each place not despoiled by us or catastrophe conveys such richness as we can never fully grasp. We feel sorry for the lowly worm, the tiny insect, the blind or deaf creatures until we realize that each slice of the world has its own glory. We are blessed certainly to sense a range of scales, augmented by our technologies, that few other species can appreciate.

Yet we must wonder whether this world is made for protoplasm, especially in its unarmored form. All the harms to which earthly flesh is heir to – disease, predation, accident, natural catastrophe, conflict – make our pathetically naked state vulnerable. As individuals we are constantly at risk of misfortune, neatly calculated by insurance. The pain we endure may vastly overtake the magic we feel until we question how this came to be and whether it is worth enduring. Fear that any hypothetical will strike us or our loved ones may consume us. We become besieged inside as fear gallops past reason and gobbles up sane territory, leaving within us a weaker frame on which to hang our hopes.

A prayer book meditation on death compares us favorably to a rock. The rock knows no wonder, the book says; it can experience neither joy and pleasure nor sadness and pain. Rather be alive with all its vicissitudes of emotional states and physical dangers than be inert like a rock, it says. Accepting our fleshly demise is compensated by all that we can feel before. The rock does have staying power, for sure. It will last longer than any of us if left lying in nature. It will feel no pain if it cracks through weathering, or when it tumbles farther down a hill, or when it ultimately gets subducted, melted, and metamorphosed deep under. But it will not experience life as only an alive creature can.

And that experience can be... exhilarating! – watching the clouds in their myriad forms throughout the day, and from above them as no person ever saw before aviation; the sparkle of light on snow, water, and trees; the glow of brownstone and graceful skyscrapers in evening light; the fellowship of good friends and new acquaintances; the accomplishment of work and personal endeavors; the raising of children to adults and the values imbued; the partners, relationships, and loves that go right and the good times with those that don't – if we are blessed to have these opportunities and not to endure constant hardship.

Oh, but the pain, and the fear that follows, swallowing up joy and wonder, turning curiosity into dread. We are so frail, bones often broken, skin easily torn, healing so long. No matter all the safety measures and warnings of civilization, which has added dangers as it has eradicated others; peril still abounds. We traded being prey to wild animals to being victim to our brethren. Our inventions become tools of misuse, corruption, scams. Disease proliferates in different forms as we create new ones from our lifestyles, technologies, and disruption of the natural world. At a certain point we lose control of our bodies, which bend to small maladies and succumb finally to large ones.

When all this overwhelms we may grow fearful, even phobic. We see ourselves in a vast universe that cares not for our solar system, much less for us. Panic in the face of the moon, the poet said. Existential terror from our being, alone in the endless reaches of dark matter, feeling precarious everywhere and nowhere to escape. Envy the rock. Phobias grow up like fungi to protect us from madness, encompassing the fearful unknown so we can still function in the rest of space... until they overtake us everywhere. Then we doubt everything about ourselves, the security and warmth we felt before, our capacity to cope. The ending looms large, always frightening but now a relief from the anxiety and pain of being... alive.

Yet, I am often quietly ecstatic and energized to be. I wouldn't trade the sublimity for anything; not the endless repose of eternity, not the fear-less state of rock. As sentient, vulnerable beings we must expect both ends of the dynamic. Temper the joy with realism. Mitigate the pain with pleasure. And avoid black holes and corners where adjustments can't be made.

When young I pitied my siblings that I had a deep love for music and they did not. I didn't countenance other, similar pleasures they undoubtedly had, and contentedly felt secure in my newfound passion. Not long after, fear and phobias shrunk my joy and confidence. I stared at the lunar eclipse from a bridge I could barely cross. Entire pathways and haunts became inaccessible. But music, visual beauty, and pleasures of the arts, sciences, and mind remained strong.

I have coped, but as I grow older I worry that fear will become dominant, as it often does with age. The joy of being, now of limited duration, smacks against the certainty of coming demise. Fantasies of ashes strewn in once-favorite places – who are they kidding? What will happen to my being… will it, unhinged from the terrestrial, reach farther into the universe? I don't believe in the afterward, yet fear of nothingness is greater than fear of being. I must be stoic, and revel in the existence I am miraculously afforded – even in the face of so much I don't understand, and the anxiety of my transient human condition.

And Finally

WHAT IS IT ABOUT?

With all the wonders, mysteries, complexities, joys, pleasures, pains, hardships, sensations, fascinations, puzzles, whimsies, and absurdities of life discussed in previous pages, do we know what this is all about? why we are here? what we are accomplishing by being alive on Earth?

These are not good questions to ask, we are told, explicitly or by shunning implication. Even modern philosophers avoid them as improper because unanswerable. Asking about the meaning of life is an adolescent exercise for late nights, before the real world of jobs and family and money come into play. No one can possibly give answers, certainly not for everyone else; only prophets, charlatans, and madmen claim otherwise. As Camus maintained, there is no meaning to life, just meanings we make for ourselves.

But underneath this protective shield, we all want to know – if we allow ourselves to think about it. In suffering we seek answers such as these, while in happiness we coast along. In moments when we consider our term on Earth, and when we observe the termination of others, we may consider how our lives fit into a broader scheme. Moreover, having a sense of purpose in life, a belief that it is all for a good reason, can be essential for our well-being. We can appreciate all the individual meanings, but particularly in times of stress and soul-searching these may not be enough.

When young I took for granted that life has an overall meaning. Growing up in post-war mid-century with its complacent security, together with the assurance of a progressive outlook from family and community, bred a near rock-solid faith in life's purpose. This began to crack as family and national troubles developed concomitantly with adolescence. College education – or, as e e cummings wrote, uneducation – further eroded these certainties. Camus's meanings became a comfortable fallback, now that the larger picture had become frayed.

Yet still, long past those tumultuous times and into other ones, I resist the notion that it is all an accident. Not that the wondrous biological creation of Earth and its inhabitants did not evolve through the workings of near-endless time and, yes, by innumerable accidents, but also by compulsion to survive or all would revert to chemical soup. But that behind all this mass of the universe, whether near-infinite in dimension or infinitesimal before the bang, there is nothing at all, just matter and energy and their unknown variants in whatever dimension, endlessly recycling over a time dimension they create in certain manifestations. That, to paraphrase the genius who understood these things better than anyone, the universe works like a roll of the dice, over and over again.

If so, then we are truly an accident, perhaps one of many such around the universe, and all that we do derives of our own device, including morality, truth, integrity, and their opposites. Then meanings are everything, good and bad, and the majority's strictures set the bounds on what is acceptable. This is not an intolerable situation; it is, in effect, the world we operate in every day. But it fails to tell us why we exist in the first place. The question is not just whether to be, for the meanings take care of that, but whether being should be taken all that seriously.

It should, although leavened with a sense of the absurd. I believe there is meaning out there, as well as in here, in our minds and hearts. While morality may be a human construct, the capacity for moral or ethical behavior and for love is not strictly human. There is evidence that other animals are capable of altruism and certainly of love. Not every human displays these traits, nor every species – nor, likely, every alien being that may exist in the universe. But the profusion of love and morality on Earth over the ages strongly suggests that they have a *universal* quality, that there is a propensity in the universe for love and the behavior it induces. This may have been what Plato meant by his eternal Forms and particularly by the overarching Form of the Good.

I posit an expansion of the universal value of good to include creativity and reflective thinking. These are not necessarily present everywhere, in every organism, or in every world. They have been part of human culture since pre-historic times – cave paintings demonstrate creativity and likely reflection as well. We may laugh at cartoons showing our companion animals thinking in human terms, but our observations of them reveal a thought process just the same; it is unlikely that many wild species do not have this capacity, too. New research on certain animal species also shows the capacity for creative thinking to solve problems. All these qualities tend to keep cropping up on our Earth, and there is no reason they couldn't happen elsewhere.

That the universe has a propensity for good and for self-fulfillment may just be an article of faith. In fairness, the idea may be as wishful as the notion of life after death. Certainly, all these traits exalted as "universal" may be explained as natural products of evolution and the survival of species. Even morality and love have survival value in protecting the social group so as to better propagate the species. But love often goes far beyond what is needed for survival, as do thought, creativity, and morality. Moreover, we *feel* that these values are right and fundamental to our existence. This feeling may simply be an evolutionary device to motivate these values – or it may signify something much bigger.

Not being a prophet (nor, I hope, a charlatan or madman), I do not assert this feeling and the idea behind it as *the* truth. It makes sense in my life, and in some form it has resonated in me since my earliest days. It explains, far beyond my upbringing or cultural derivation, why certain values hold fast within me. I wouldn't be devastated if it weren't so; we do function pretty well under the social contract that includes many of these values. But the concept of a universal propensity for good and other fulfilling values certainly adds comfort if not security to our lives. What really holds out there we have yet to discover, if we ever do. As I wrote earlier in these pages, life is full of mysteries.

CPSIA information can be obtained
at www.ICGtesting.com
Printed in the USA
BVHW040846010519
547054BV00021B/571/P